*Parenting*
# YOUR
# TEEN
## WITHOUT
## LOSING YOUR
*Cool*

TORONTO

"This read was a complete eye-opener. There has never been a more petrifying time to raise teens. In a world where external influences and pressures are at its peak, coupled with the increase in teen anxiety and depression, it's imperative that we educate ourselves on what's really going on and learn how to better navigate the challenges at hand. Shantelle's book does just that."

*–Nina Purewal, International Bestselling Author of Let That Sh\*t Go.*
*@nina.pure.minds*

"The real gift of this book is its gentle invitation for parents to explore their fears of the teenage years and feel guided through them in the way that only earned and learned wisdom can.

In Shantelle's signature compassionate transparency, she lays out what it was like, what she'd do differently, and the hard but right parenting decisions she made to truly raise her kids without losing her cool.

It feels like you're talking to a girlfriend who's been there and who has time to listen to what's on your heart about the decade we paint as a four-letter word, and in doing so, she makes it a lot less scary."

*–Leisse Wilcox, Conscious relationship coach, mentor*
*and best-selling author of To Call Myself Beloved. @leissewilcox*

"As a single mother of four kids, I need this book. Like, I really must read and refer back to this book. Having survived raising an emotionally intelligent and reasonably competent eighteen-year-old daughter, I'm in a completely different space with my three boys. I wonder if we will be friends at all! I love Shantelle's frankness because we are in a time of needing the simple truth. There were so many valuable reminders that I needed to hear and insights I hadn't appreciated. After reading, I feel equipped to stay on course and can now see a thriving future for my boys and me."

"As the parent of six teens and tweens, I know firsthand the challenges that parents face. For any parents who are feeling overwhelmed, scared, and alone, this is the book for you! The teen years can present a number of parenting firsts that we didn't necessarily consider when we signed up for having our babies. With the guidance, understanding, and practical tips provided in this book, you will learn how to enjoy these special developmental years with your children while remaining level-headed!"

# Parenting YOUR TEEN WITHOUT LOSING YOUR Cool

A SURVIVAL GUIDE TO GET *you* THROUGH THE TEEN YEARS, ALIVE.

Shantelle Bisson

*Parenting Your Teen Without Losing Your Cool:*
*A Survival Guide to Get You Through the Teen Years, Alive*

Copyright @ 2021 Shantelle Bisson

YGTMedia Co. Press Trade Paperback Edition

ISBN trade paperback: 978-1-989716-21-2

eBook: 978-1-989716-22-9

Audio book: 978-1-989716-23-6

Published in Canada, for Global Distribution

by YGTMedia Co.

www.ygtmama.com/publishing

To order additional copies of this book: publishing@ygtmama.com

Developmental Editing by Tania Jane Moraes-Vaz
Edited by Christine Stock
Book design by Doris Chung
Cover design by Michelle Fairbanks
ePub & Kindle editions by Ellie Silpa

Printed in North America

For my mother, who managed to somehow keep her cool during my teen years even though I was an absolute pain in the ass *and* made her a grandmother at 37.

I love you!

To Brianna, Dominique, and Mikaela, my strong, bold, fearless, patient, and wonderful daughters. Thank you for forgiving me for all the ways I completely blew it during your teen years. You've taught me so much, and I'm blessed to be your mom. Thank you for choosing me.

This book is because of you, and for you.

Love,
Mutti

# Contents

# INTRODUCTION

I'm not sure how you got here with my book about parenting your teens in your hot little hands. Perhaps you've seen me on TV, talking about my book *Raising Your Kids Without Losing Your Cool*, and you agreed with my parenting techniques and thought you could use some help with the alien who has taken over your once joyful, easygoing child. Maybe you read my book on kids because you have a mixed bag of ages running through your home, some in the kid zone and some in the tween/teen zone. And now you're moving on, continuing your parenting education. Perhaps you purchased my first book, thinking it covered all the years of raising your kid, and you were pissed that it didn't. You may have even felt ripped off—I include this assumption because this sort of grumbling did get back to me a time or two; but, as your friend, you have to know that if I had told you about blow-job parties, self-harm, and the possibility of your kids being approached on the internet about being somebody's sugar baby, all while advising you to not lose your cool over a gender-reveal party, you would have had a heart attack before even getting to the delivery of your new family member. So, I did you a favor by separating these books into two.

Trust me.

Or maybe you buy books the way I buy books—you wander the bookstore aisles aimlessly, waiting for your next "must-have" to jump off the shelf at you. Or maybe, just maybe, you're at the end of your rope with a super miserable home situation, and you've already read every parenting blog and followed dozens of moms on Instagram, looking for advice, guidance, support and, let's be honest, some #momtruths to remind you that you're not actually going crazy, you're just going through a crazy time.

Whatever your reason for picking up my book, I'm thankful you're here. I may not have a whole whack of letters after my name, but what I do have is invaluable—I've been there, done that . . . three times. Like you, I spent many dark days in the pit with an all-encompassing fear that I would never, ever in a million fucking lifetimes get to the other side of my mom journey. There were days, if I'm being brutally honest with you, that I was confident that one of us wouldn't come out of the teen years alive. It was either going to be one of them, or me, but one thing was for sure: It wouldn't be both of us. Of this, I was certain. I mean, talk about getting to the ultimate losing-your-cool thinking!

But hey, what can I say? Such is life when parenting teens.

While I was in the thick of it, I can honestly say that there were many days when I actually thought I could not go one step further. I felt like I needed to cut loose and run. And the worst part of those days when I was out of my depth and overwhelmed, confused, and exhausted was that there was no one I could really lean on. It wasn't that I didn't have friends; I had plenty. But many of them had no kids, so even though I could share what I was going through, they didn't get it. And my friends who also had teens? Well, let's just say we found it easier to discuss our sex lives than really share what our kids were going through or what we were going through as parents. Being a parent to a teen during the teen years was, for me, an extremely lonely time, and since you have this book in your hands, I'd venture a guess that you, too, are in the middle of your own moment of "What the fuck is going on and what am I supposed to do next?" Like me, you and your girlfriends stopped talking about Bobby's poops and Jenny's dance classes a long time ago, and now you won't dare broach the subject of their possible eating disorder or casual drug use that might not be quite so casual anymore.

And that's where I come in. I've written this book for you with the hope that it will offer you some peace of mind so you know that even though it feels like you're living in an alternate universe with your alien child, you're not alone. Now that the days of posting all the sweet nothings and cute singing and dancing videos of your mini-me, who wears what you tell them to and says what you want them to, are behind you, perhaps you feel like you're at the end of your rope and are wondering, *Crap, now what?* You're in need of some support, some help, some truth, some hang time with a woman who went through a lot of the things and made it out alive. If I can do it, you can too! And just as I did in my first book on parenting kids, I'm here to give you some tools to not only survive

> I'm here to give you some tools to not only survive the teen years but to thrive through them.

♡

the teen years but to *thrive* through them. I give you what you need to talk through the difficult moments. I guide you in helping them through shitty breakups and getting them the help they need should they develop an eating disorder, plus I give you info on how to help them understand their sexual urges/tendencies and how to determine if they're participating in self-harm.

Yeah, I'm here to be that friend who will talk to you about anything and everything you may be dealing with these next few years. We will get a strategy in place for dealing with and addressing shit like drugs, and how to support whatever gender your teen chooses to identify by. I suggest some books that were absolute game changers for me and let you know when to consider therapy as the best option for both of you. I also provide you with the skills to teach them how to stand up under peer pressure and how to do the right thing when their crew wants them to do what's wrong.

I've done it. My girls have grown up as the first generation of social media users and have never been nude on the internet (well, not that I know of) or been paid by some creepy old dude asking them to sell him photos of their feet. If you think kids aren't out there making money this way, then you need this book more than I thought you did because yes, these situations happen all day, every day, and they are sometimes much worse. In fact, this weird and creepy trend is on the rise, and I don't know where you live, or what's happening in your part of the world, but there is even a ranking system that reveals which universities and colleges have the highest per capita of sugar babies in their student body.

Wow, right?!

Shit's crazy, for sure! I mean, what happened to kids having part-time jobs like scooping ice cream or serving coffee at their local café or working at the grocery store? The world your teen is growing up in is not the world we grew up in. It's a totally different beast now, and if you want to get your teen to the other side intact, then let me, a woman who knows how to avoid the landmines, help you navigate your route.

I don't know your story; maybe you always wanted to be a mother, perhaps you were president of the PTA or head volunteer and did all those good parenting deeds, but now your kid won't let you drive them to school anymore. You may also already be at that stage where they stay behind a closed door most of the time or live their lives in their phones. You feel lost and alone and out of your depth as you head into these teen years. Your teen's angst hurls a wrench into your parenting confidence, and you're on the brink of throwing in the emotional towel and leaving them to their own devices because honestly, it just seems simpler than constantly being at war. I know that feeling of dread. I've been there too.

Or you may be in the tween years, and your kid is still groovy, life is still blissful and lovely, and you grabbed my book because you want to get a jump on the teen years that are coming down the pipe. Whatever stage of your parenting journey you find yourself in, I want you to know, with confidence, that the challenges will reap great rewards. There are a lot of amazing moments coming your way. There is an abundance of joy headed for you as you witness your little person become their own free-thinking, independent person. And I can assure you that you will get through these teen years the way you always envisioned you would—cool. You will be the cool parent; your house will be the one where all the other kids want to hang out. And your kids will tell you things, sometimes too many things in too much detail (I can say this confidently from experience). They will want you to drop them off at school. Your kid will cry and hug you tight as you get ready to walk

> These are the years that you really need to have your wits about you.
>
> ♡

out of their dorm room for the first time, leaving them on their own.

All the cool things you always dreamed of doing with them will happen. You will parent them in such a way that at the end of the teen years, not only will you have raised an awesome human to send out into the world, you will have gained a lifelong friend. Because if the girl who got pregnant at nineteen with a boy she had known for just four months, the girl who has now crossed the thirty-three-year mark with that boy and has had three daughters with him—if she could get the job done with the odds heavily stacked against her, you can too.

My husband, Yannick, and I were both from broken homes. He had lived on his own from the tender age of fifteen, and I lived with a dad who spent my entire young life coming and going until he finally left for good when I was thirteen. My mother, a single parent, did all she could to give me a normal life, but it was tough. I was a pain in the ass. I didn't make life easy for her, yet she didn't waver. She stayed her parenting course, and because of it, I was able to do the same with my three girls. My husband, however, left to his own devices, parented himself through his teen years, as a teen . . . weird, right? There were so many things we had to overcome as humans, never mind as parents. Then you, who I'm assuming had a better jumping off point than we did, can totally and absolutely get across the finish line intact. And happy. And grateful. And fucking cool, without ever losing your cool.

So, let's be honest with each other here, since we're officially friends, thanks to you buying my book. It's super easy to parent a child when you lay out their clothes every night and they eagerly wear them. Or when they let you cut their hair the way you think looks cutest. And when they say yes to the activities you've put them in. Or when they let you post them on your Instagram and happily do TikTok dances with you. It's easy when you're in control, and they don't have voices, opinions, ideas, and attitudes of their own. It's all fun and games until the first time they call you a bitch, or a dick, or worse, tell you to fuck off.

You don't see parents posting those family videos to their social media, now do you?

No, you don't. These are the years that you really need to have your wits about you. These are the years that you need to have a plan, a course of action for any and *all* possible outcomes and outbursts. I will help you be prepared for the battle that lies before you.

These years will be some of your greatest. You will witness your teens accomplish incredible things and develop strong characteristics and personalities. There will be blissful moments that may sometimes be overshadowed by the dark ones.

But you can do it.

You will do it.

I know you will, because if I did it and came out smiling on the other side, you can too. We'll get through it together. But keep this thought in mind: You are not always going to be "IN" love with your kid, but you will *always* love them. You won't always be thankful that you had your kid, when the shit is hitting the fan. But in the end, that kid will become one of your favorite people.

This book will give you the tools you need to get through all the challenges of being a parent of a teen without losing your cool.

You can trust me on this claim. I've gone to battle, I've slain some rather nightmarish demons, and I've won the war. And now I want to help you do the same. So, let's do this . . . *TOGETHER*.

# THE ELEPHANT IN THE ROOM: PARENTING DURING A GLOBAL PANDEMIC

Before we get into the guts of this book, I can't not touch on this one topic: the COVID-19 pandemic.

Lockdowns.

Quarantines.

All the things.

When I sat down to write this book, I was on the fence as to whether I would address the elephant in the room in all our lives, the globe over: being a parent during the first global pandemic of our lifetimes. I thought by the time this book hit the shelves we would be so far on the other side of it, and I didn't want to trigger any PTSD for you. But this so isn't the case. Unfortunately.

Somehow, more than a year later, we're still being tossed back and forth between lockdowns and homeschooling, which is now what we refer to as "normal" living. I also wrestled with whether I wanted to date this book in that way. Someone who buys it five, ten, twenty years from now may not want to go back down that road, or maybe they lived in a part of the world, like Australia or New Zealand, where after the first phase of COVID-19, life returned to "normal" fairly quickly. I was a yo-yo of *do I or do I not add a chapter about what is possibly a transformational time for many?*

With my brilliant editor's insight, we decided to put it in here because, well, quite frankly, this pandemic changed every single one of us to the very core of our being. We, as a society, as humans, will never be the same again. And in some ways, I'm all for it. Like, can we please keep the number of people allowed on one elevator car to two or a maximum of four persons if they are all from the same household? I'm loving that! Or how about keeping six feet back from other people in lines? And how about respecting personal space? Let's TOTALLY keep that one! To be honest, I've never fully understood how crawling up my ass in an already-crowded space ever expedited a line, like EVER. And what about the changes to the environment? How about the fact that the canals in Venice are clear again? How about the replantation of the Great Barrier Reef? For the first time, there are no crowds of tourists tarnishing the ecological footprint. The list of pluses goes on and on. There's a lot to celebrate for sure, but as it always is with life, there will forever be the opposite side of the shiny coin. It's not always a win-win situation. And for parents and teens the world over, there was, unfortunately, very little winning.

My girls are all adults. So, as a parent to a teen, you might be thinking, "Lucky you. At least they were independent, out of the house, established in their own lives."

Not so fast, friend.

This past year, my eldest got pregnant, then miscarried. Due to pandemic restrictions on in-person visits, it was difficult for me to arrange to see her and care for her during that emotional and painful time. Thankfully, she had her husband by her side, but moms should be allowed to be with their children during times of crises, and this pandemic stole that from me and so many other parents—parents of sick children who needed surgery or were diagnosed with cancer, parents of kids who were alone as they fought for their lives. There has been so much suffering for so many families, no matter the family dynamic or demographic, that some may never fully recover.

Our middle girl had to move back in with us in Los Angeles. She is a stylist who primarily dresses rappers, but because there were no tours, and not many music videos being produced, there was no work to be had. This lack of work was demoralizing for her. She was twenty-nine and finally living on her own, and she had to come back under our roof. I'm happy to report now that by the time this book went to press, she's back out on her own!

Our youngest, who lives with us, struggled (like I did) with going to that really dark place of fearing certain death that the news kept shoving down our throats, and both of us found it hard in the beginning to be calm and live normally within the "new normal." Eventually, we got our feet under us, and as we learned more about the virus, we were able to let go and live more freely—still carefully, but definitely with less anxiety tied to our every move we made outside of our own four walls.

We've all struggled and gotten through this pandemic as best we can. Some introverts couldn't be happier about the freedom to stay home. To stay put. To cocoon with their favorite person/persons. I have a good friend who is thriving, has never felt better, is less stressed out, and has even fallen madly in love. But the experiences that most of us have had over the past year couldn't be more polarizing. And one thing is for certain: If you ask any teen you know (and I've talked to quite a few of the teens who work for me at my marina), life has been extremely weird and stressful. The general consensus is that everybody is just hoping that life doesn't go on this way forever. There are many teens who have missed their first year of high school or their last, their first dance or their senior prom. There are university students who haven't been able to walk across the stage to receive their degree, culminating eighteen years of hard work. There have been so many firsts and lasts stolen from millions and millions of future adults. Childhood, tween-hood, teenage years, and the initiation into young adulthood have been forever changed.

So, now what? How do you parent a teen who is heading into the second year of lost moments? Because we adults all know that the one thing we can never get back once it's gone is TIME.

The pain that surfaces from the loss of these social and pivotal milestones has caused a great number of teens to withdraw. And others, who were already high risk and have a tendency to self-harm, may consider suicide. The statistics aren't out yet, and we may never get them—perhaps because our governments don't want us to know the depth of loss due to the strain the lockdowns have put on vulnerable teens' mental wellness—but my guess is there has been a massive spike in teen suicides this past year. And if you're reading these words, and you have lost a child to suicide or know somebody who has, I take this moment to genuinely wrap you in love and offer you my deepest, most sincere condolences for the loss of your perfect, beautiful child. I cannot even begin to fathom the depth of pain that is left behind by this sort of loss. My heart is completely and entirely with you.

Truly.

Now, here we are. It is 2021, and we're in year two of this thing, and we may or may not have collected an arsenal of tools to make this second go-around better than the first. Or perhaps you're done. Your tank is empty, and your battery has zero charge left. Wherever you are in your journey of pandemic parenting, I want to first congratulate you for doing something that has rarely been done before—parenting a teen while trying to keep your own mental health in order, or trying to hold onto your job (and maybe everything else), or mourning the loss of a loved one, all a result of the pandemic. This past year has been an emotionally charged and unimaginable time in all our lives, and I legitimately salute you for getting here. Wherever you are right now, in this moment, reading this book, I want you to celebrate yourself. You have done it. You are surviving something none of us had any tools for when it first came for us, and I'm proud of you.

Like wildly proud of you.

It was hard for me with three adult daughters, but I didn't have to homeschool. I didn't have to hold them while they cried about missing their circle of friends, while they struggled to self-motivate themselves to get their schoolwork done, or while they missed out on opportunities for university scholarships for the sports they played, perfected, and worked at for their entire lives.

Much about being a parent has changed this past year—almost every damn thing! We've learned a lot about ourselves and have come to realize how capable we are with our innate ability to pivot in nearly every single area of our lives. We've come to learn that we are way fucking stronger than we ever imagined we would need to be. Some people have left marriages that were not healthy, fulfilling, or loving. Others left jobs that didn't serve their greatest good so they could be home to care for their kids or finally start that business they've been wanting to open. And yet others stopped juggling a crippling and soul-sucking

> There has been very little in our kids' lives that hasn't been affected by the pandemic.

♡

job with a budding side gig and went all in on their dreams so they could be there for their families and live in moments that lit them up every day, even during a pandemic. Whatever growth came out of this year, chances are lots of it wouldn't have happened without the pandemic forcing our hands as it did and still does. And as some things might have changed for us, I believe the lives of our teens were entirely changed. There has been very little in our kids' lives that hasn't been affected by the pandemic.

I want you to take a few moments to close your eyes and think about what possibly stayed the same for your teen this year, and please feel free to DM me your findings, because I will go out on a limb here and say that few things remained the same. They've lost a lot—their sports, their social lives, their educations, and for some, their homes. Their entire lives have been rocked.

So, where do we—you and I—go from here? If you happened to read my first book, you'll know how against social media I am. You'll know why I think kids should have their screen time heavily monitored. You should know where they're going/hanging out when they have it and for how long they are on it. The same advice applies for online gaming. But what's a parent to do when so many teens the world over now spend their entire lives inside their homes with just you? Well, for starters, you need to put the past behind you—all the mistakes and missteps—and begin anew. Holding on to the past will not serve you, and I get it. The years 2020 and 2021 have not been very kind to us as a whole. So, the only way we can respond to that is to work harder to be even kinder. What's that expression? *Don't let it make you bitter, allow it to make you better?* Or something like that? Hopefully, friends, this message is what my book helps you accomplish, pandemic parenting and all. I'm here to guide you through these years with your sanity, and theirs, in check!

*Chapter One*

# BEFORE THE CLOCK STRIKES TEEN

Ticktock, TikTok . . . and yes, pun very much intended! Teen years today look and feel much different than perhaps what you and I experienced. Still, you've made it this far, navigating the roller coaster of ever-fluctuating hormones, growth spurts, and all the rites of passage that come with being a teenager. You've gone from birth to double digits, and you may have heeded the advice offered in my first book, *Raising Your Kids Without Losing Your Cool*, to get you to this point. And if you've grabbed this book and are in the homestretch with one final tween and a whole whack of teens already residing under your roof, then do nothing else with your time until you read this book and start putting my advice into practice, pronto.

Alright, if you're reading this book, it's because you have successfully survived the first decade of parenting. Yay, you! I am so fucking proud of you; parenting is not for the faint of heart, and yet here you are! You must know that you're a living, breathing rock star / demigod! You totally know this, right? Now, I happen to be extremely confident because I've been exactly where you are, and I know that there were probably a gazillion times along the way when you wanted to tap out, yet you didn't. By now I hope you also know that it is completely normal to have felt like you were going out of your mind a time or two, or five thousand! It's also absolutely normal to have felt unsure of the choices you made in raising your kid. Trust me when I tell you that you are not alone. Like SO. NOT. ALONE.

I have good news and bad news for you . . . let me give you the bad news first. If you thought the first ten years kicked your ass, I hope you're prepared for an entirely different set of challenges with this next phase of your parenting journey: the tween and teen years. Because we're officially best friends, and I swore to tell you the whole truth and nothing but the truth, I have to tell you that there is like a 99.9 percent chance that they will be much more difficult than the first ten were. The good news? If you put in the work, all the work, no shortcuts, then you will come out the other side with human beings you're obsessed with, that you want to spend almost every waking moment with, and who feel the exact same way about you!

For me, I have two visuals in my head of what being a parent is like. 1) I'm not a video game playing sort of person, and only one of my girls was ever into them, so I don't know much about them. But what little I do know is this: In every single video game, the player is always trying to get to the next level. They never know what lies around the next corner (I already run anxious, so I don't need any video game to add to my made-up end-of-the-world bullshit I have going on in my head . . . but I digress), which causes their heart to race with adrenaline. It's always exciting, and it's always challenging, and if you love that sort of cortisol flight-or-fight way of living, then you'll totally love parenting! 2) Or how about this other analogy that I love: Parenting is like putting IKEA furniture together . . . all the pieces are present but there are only squiggly drawings instructing how to build a bookcase that can withstand the weight of the world (aka your books). You're not quite sure if it's all going to work out, but now you're in it and there's no turning back until you get to the next level or get that bookshelf put together. The investment of time and energy has been made, and nobody quits when the level gets too hard or when the shelf is nearly complete. If either one of these scenarios gets you excited, then you, my friend, don't even need this book because you are a prime candidate for parenting!

But if you're like me, not really sure you were ever going to procreate but went for it anyway, you now spend more of your time feeling like you're doing it wrong, especially as you embark on what I like to call your child's gap years when you're both just trying to figure out who you want to be in this new relationship dynamic. Does your kid want to stay like a "baby" or run full steam ahead into teendom? Not even your kid will know what they want during this hormonal,

> Not even your kid will know what they want during this hormonal, awkward, who-the-hell-am-I time.

awkward, who-the-hell-am-I time. In fact, your unique mini-you may bounce between the two daily, or hourly, or, in some cases, minutes. I know. Daunting and horrifying, but true! Whatever level of possession has taken over your kid, you gotta keep your eye on the prize and remember what skills got you here to double digits: you were prepared, you were organized, you had structure, and most importantly, you were unified with your partner. You also had strong, clear, open, and humble communication with your child, and you were consistent with them. All this good, juicy stuff is exactly what is going to get you through any rough patches coming your way over the next several years. If you see yourself in this description, then you need this book. You need me to be your friend.

Trust me when I tell you this: I know without a shadow of a doubt that you're going to get to the other side. Don't fear—prepare. Don't doubt—believe. You didn't only live through the first decade, you totally killed it! Now, here you are, ten years in. TEN YEARS! You are doing AWESOME! You went from knowing nothing to having a decade of parenting under your belt. If you got here with *zero* experience, think about how great you are going to be now that you have that knowledge, that success, and all those victories behind you. Experience makes us more confident, am I right? You know that I am! You're going to continue to do awesome because now we have one another, and I'm totally with you. You're going to lose your cool, but that's absolutely normal and fine because I'm going to help you learn how to regain it. You've acquired tons of organizational skills from having littles, and now you're just going to expand on all that goodness. You're going to continue to admit when you've blown it, you're going to say you're sorry before you're asked to, then you're going to let go and move the fuck on. That's really what parenting is all about. Hell, it's what life is all about. When you're faced with something you know nothing about, or a situation that is out of your scope of knowledge, you can't just turn your back on it or put your head in the sand and hope for the best, even if that would feel awesome on some days. I speak honestly because I spent a fair amount of time with my head in the sand or in my pjs in bed with what I like to call "the parenting flu." Sometimes it's just all too much. Sometimes you just need a break from the exhausting madness that comes with being consistent in your parenting. And hey, that's OKAY. Hell, it's more than okay; it's essential to your mental wellness. Taking days off when you need them is totally key to making it through this lifelong job you've taken on. You can check out from time to time, but only if you promise me that you will *always* check back in.

You promise?

You swear to me that you will?

I mean, you wouldn't bullshit me now, would you? 'Cause that would be a really terrible way to start a brand-new friendship.

Alright, cool, I'm glad we cleared that up.

Ready to dig in and start laying the groundwork for a strong relationship in the teen years?

I am! Let's do this!

## KEEPING YOUR COOL WHEN YOU FEEL ANYTHING BUT COOL

Listen, **I get it**—parenting is a huge amount of pressure placed on your shoulders. You are responsible for raising this child into a mighty grown-up. You must seek out solutions and support, which is what you did when your child went from being a small person to blasting into the double digits. It seems like only yesterday you were breastfeeding your baby, and now you're already having conversations about if ten is too young to shave legs, or if your son would please, just please use tissues instead of his socks when masturbating. Yes. It all moves that swiftly. A decade sounds like a long time, and it is until you're a parent in charge of molding a new human. You now have a tween in your household, and you're officially embarking on the tween years. These are the years I like to refer to as the "exorcist" years. You're going to need a lot of wine, whiskey, tequila—take your pick or rotate through them all—whatever gets you through, and you're also going to need to be patient and firm. You'll still have those moments when your tween will want to snuggle up with you and have you read them a bedtime story, and then there will be some nights when that same sweet cherub slams their bedroom door in your face, yelling that they just wish you would leave them alone! It's going to feel like you live in another dimension. You'll probably even look up in the corners of your hallways or behind plants because you're totally confident you're being punked, and it will 1,000 percent cause you to doubt yourself. And it will absolutely, beyond the shadow of a doubt, take a wrecking ball to your partnership. The downside? Your wrecking ball won't have a hot Miley Cyrus straddling and singing on it.

Being so destabilized due to this alien living in your house will create different visceral reactions in both you and your partner. When our girls got to the Linda Blair years, their behavior made my husband and me wonder if we had done even one thing right, it totally put us on edge, and it had us arguing ad nauseum over who had the best plan of attack on how to deal with the shitty attitudes being flung at us 24/7. Something that made me see red had zero negative effect on him, and vice versa. In the end our conclusion was that we were doing just fine and, for that wild and insane time, doing just fine was good enough for us!

So, be like us. Let go and just trust yourself, trust the work you've put in, trust the respectful foundation you have built between parent and child, then march on in this battle, ready to produce a well-rounded, strong, intelligent human who will go out into the world and be a wonderful and productive addition to society. Keep your cool, even when you feel like you've totally lost it. Keep the communication lines open with your partner, even if by this stage in raising your kids you're no longer residing under one roof. It's important to remember that you're still a parenting team. Get unified, if you haven't done so already. If you have, and you and your ex are grooving along in your parenting journey, then you can skip ahead to the next section.

> Keep your cool, even when you feel like you've totally lost it.

To the couples who are no longer connected in an intimate way and are no longer living under one roof with their kids, let's have a frank conversation about the best way to ensure your kids have healthy teen years, regardless of your relationship status. Let's not forget that it took both of you to create this person, and it requires both of you to raise them. One of the mistakes a separated couple can no longer face together is when one parent completely checks out. My dad checked out, both emotionally and financially—like, who doesn't call their child on her Sweet Sixteen? Remember that a breakup of parents is not the kids' fault, so play nice with your ex and always be a parent to your children. Also keep in mind here, parents, that you not getting along with your ex-partner is a drag for your children as well as the parent who gets stuck doing all the heavy lifting on their own. So, if you're in separate homes, then I implore you to make a pact, no matter how ugly the breakup (although if there was an abusive situation, then keep your children as far away from that parent as humanly and legally possible to do so). But let's assume here that the relationship simply didn't work out and you came to realize that you just weren't each other's person.

That's cool.

You're not the only one at all. However (and I cannot stress this enough), as a kid who found it pretty awful to be "dumped" by my father the second he moved in with his new woman and then started to have more kids, I need you to get your ex to agree that they will always be an equal partner in the parenting of your children. You will need this unity. It's easier to level the battlefield when the two of you team up. Two is greater than one, especially during the transition years from child to teen, then teen to young adult, then adult to . . . well, life. You will need to be a team for the rest of your lives, and this isn't your children's problem. They didn't ask to be born; you did the thing, and you owe it to them to raise them well and to get along.

If you can manage to get along and co-parent without involving a couple's counselor or, even better, without involving a lawyer, I encourage you to work out how that looks for both of you. Does it mean you have a Bat phone for reaching the other parent at any hour of the day or night when it pertains to something going on with your offspring?

I don't know. I wasn't in your partnership. But I can tell you that it makes all the difference in the world as to how your kid gets through life/teendom knowing that both parents are paying attention. Both are invested. Both are as committed to keeping their cool as much as they did

> It makes all the difference in the world as to how your kid gets through life knowing that both parents are paying attention.

before the breakup and before your child hit double digits.

What I recall more than anything about my parents' breakup was how my dad simply vanished. His disappearing out of our lives triggered a domino effect of traumas for my mother, me, and my two brothers. The biggest was the eviction from our family home. We had to move in with my grandmother in her two-bedroom house. My mom and I slept in a small room on a pullout couch, my brothers slept in the basement on a pullout couch, and we had one bathroom between five of us. It was traumatic leaving our home and all our stuff behind, and I don't feel as if my father cared that he had put us in this position. Not one bit.

Don't be *that* parent in the breakdown of a relationship. Regardless of how your relationship ends, the one you have with your children lasts a lifetime. Be your best self in the breakup; your kids deserve it. After all, there is no kid on the planet who asked to be born, to be brought into your lives—*you decided* to have children. You made them. You added them to your lives. So, no matter what happens in your intimate partnership, it should not roll downhill onto your children. Step up and make the vow to always do right by your kids.

Should you find yourself at the breaking point of your relationship, honor and provide for your children no matter what. That is on you. That is a choice you made when you opted to bring them into the world. You must see it through, no matter how angry you are at your ex. It's really quite simple, although adults do have a way of overcomplicating it. Some "adults" in these painful, upsetting situations find themselves operating from ego—from hurt, rage, jealousy, bitterness, insecurity, and more. None of it good. All these emotions, which are completely and entirely justified when you're heartbroken, eventually dissipate over time with healing and often with a newfound lover. But should you choose to be a complete asshole to your children and dump them in the thick of one or all these emotions, the uphill climb to win back your children is a long haul, my friend. My advice to you, as a grown-up who endured seven years of pain over a dad who did the least and gave the least, is this: Do everybody a favor and be the bigger person from the get-go of the end of the relationship with your ex-lover for the sake and well-being of your little people who are simply caught in the cross fire.

Alright, I'm glad we cleared all that up. Are you ready to dig into what you came here for? Help with parenting your teen? I know I am! Let's get to it!

**LAYING THE FOUNDATION**

Okay, I may lose some of you here, but I'm hoping you will stick with me and just, you know, hear me out. Some parents are going for the super-chill-parent-of-the-century award. You know, just fully flowing with whatever way the wind blows their kid. Allowing them to just chart their own course through life. No sleep schedule. No sleeping structure, aka a bedroom of their own. Never uttering the word "no," for any reason. Letting them decide what they will eat, and when. Fully embracing the whole "uninvolved parenting" vibe. And for a while it seemed cute, dreamy even. But now you're beginning to notice that what was cute, inquisitive, and free is starting to feel disrespectful, annoying, and, well, gross. What was charming and fun at age four when they would basically tell you to "mind your business" with their I-got-this-raising-myself-all-by-myself-shit-down attitude is suddenly like the proverbial nails on a chalkboard energy. And you're no fool; you know that you really need to take back the reins and get it all under control, but it's been a decade, and, well, your kid disagrees. How are you going to do it? How do you now become the parent, ten years in, that you always should have been? Well, I have to say that I'm doubtful it's going to be easy, which is why you'll never catch me doing this uninvolved parenting nonsense, but there's nothing we can do about it now—we weren't friends the first ten years. But we are now, and as your friend, I'm going to do my job to help you become the adult in your relationship because your kid is going to need you, and now is the time to get onside with your tween. The waters of teen life are going to get rough, and we need you as the captain, pronto!

If the aforementioned parenting style sounds familiar, I'm going to recommend to you and your parenting partner that you get aligned with how you are going to insert and assert yourselves as the parents at this stage in the relationship. And the way that I suggest doing it successfully has recurring themes in how I parent:

**1) Do it with humility.** Demonstrate humility with each other and with your kid. Sit them down and admit that you made a mistake by allowing them to be the boss of themselves. Explain that as they get older, there will be mature matters they will encounter that they won't have the life experience or the skill set to deal with all alone, and since you've "been there, done that," you've got a lot of wisdom, support, guidance, and love to shower on them to help them navigate these waters as smoothly as possible.

Admitting to your child that you are only human and that sometimes even as a grown-up you can make mistakes or head in a direction that isn't best for everybody is a very good lesson to teach them. When we stand up in front of our children and admit to them that we're not perfect, and we're okay with not being perfect, it allows them the strength to not only accept it within themselves but also to not freak out when that time comes for them.

**2) Get help. Set aside the martyr complex. You won't always know everything or how to swoop in and save the day. And that's okay.** If reclaiming your parenting role in your child's life is not going well, I suggest that you get help. Get help sooner than later. I'm a big fan of having an unbiased person in the parenting relationship because as cool as we think we are, our kids (and this may come as a surprise to you) likely don't agree. So, if you get to the stage where the relationship has hit an impasse, get help. It can be as easy as speaking to your child's doctor about what's going on at home, or a school guidance counselor you respect, or a friend you know your child loves, admires, and listens to. I utilized all these help lines when I was in the thick of it with my girls. If you have the means to afford professional help, then look for a psychologist who can help you set healthy parenting boundaries before it's too late. And then, like Nike says, "Just do it." Get on track of being the parent in the relationship. I'm not saying it's going to be easy to become the parent this late in the game, but I'm confident that with a lot of patience, humility, and help, you will get to the other side of taking back this role in your kid's life. How quickly you make this transition has a lot to do with a) how easygoing your kid is, and b) how consistent you are at reclaiming this role in their life. But if you want to raise an awesome human, which I know you do, I know you'll gently, lovingly, and firmly become the parent your child needs during this new phase of their life. And, my friend, I totally know that you've got this!

Get on track of being the parent in the relationship.

Right now, you may find that you haven't hit the wall with your tween, and that's awesome. I don't recall having many issues with our girls from ages ten to thirteen. We had a good flow—balance, if you will. It wasn't until after thirteen that we all started to lose the pedals, and some of us more than others. And when I say "some of us," I'm referring to mostly me. I know that I'm an emotional person. I am an idealistic individual who struggled with issues as a teen, and I was a young mom whose unresolved pieces of herself rolled downhill onto the shoulders of my unsuspecting, innocent girls. It wasn't always pretty, there was a lot of crying (mostly by me), lots of laughing (mostly them at me), and tons of saying, "I'm sorry." Again, mostly me. No one is perfect, including our tweens. Therefore, this time in your parenting requires grace—grace for your tween/teen, your partner, and yourself.

And rules. You're going to need some nonnegotiable rules.

You're not here to let your kids do something just because all the other kids are allowed to do it. Don't fall for that bullshit that kids, and myself at one time, have been handing out to their parents for *forever.* Hell, you might have even given that line to your own parents! And definitely do not crumble to parent peer pressure. How you choose to do all you can for your kid's safety is none of their business. And trust me when I tell you this: The friends you have and that your kid has going into the tween years will not be the friends that come out of the teen years with them, or you. You might get one, but that's it. So, don't parent your child to impress someone or to keep a relationship with another parent going. Your one job is to do right by your kid, which means you need to be consistent during these years more than ever. The tween/teen years are when they're really starting to flex their muscles and check out whether they can actually fly on their own. You need to be consistent—consistent with your discipline, with your rules, and with your love. They're going to test you; they're going to see if they ask you the same question for the one millionth time whether you will finally crack and say yes. They'll be casually talking to you about seemingly innocent topics while you're paying bills and then they'll slip in a question about something they know you'd always say no to, but you're just that perfect level of distracted and they're gambling on you slipping and saying yes when you mean no. PAY ATTENTION. BE ALERT. Be ready for their trickery at all times. And for the love of God, if you and your partner are still living under one roof together, you must be united as parents. You both must follow the rules that you agreed upon with your kid. You both must be loving, fair, and consistent with your kid. You didn't have your kid so you could be their friend; you had your kid to be their parent, so don't stop now.

Many parents I've talked to believe that the younger years are the toughest ones to get through, and in many ways, that is true. You're more tired, you run around to all their various activities, you work, you have sex with your partner, you manage your home, and you perhaps have other kids. Yes, the birth-to-ten years are tough, but the ten-to-eighteen years are the emotionally trying, stay-up-late-waiting-for-them-to-come-home-from-a-party-so-you-can-check-the-whites-of-their-eyes years. These are your frontline, head-above-the-trench parenting battle years, and you must be prepared. So, bask in the fact that you've come this far, and rejoice in knowing that if you've done the work leading up to this next phase of life, you will have a much more successful time. I'm not here to freak you out. I'm here to be honest with you. I'm on your side, and I want you to enjoy these next years. I want you to write me letters and emails, telling me that even though you had challenges and storms with your tween or teen, you're on the other side of it, and that yes, implementing your house rules and seeing them through laid the foundation for a beautiful relationship in which your word was ultimately final, and your kid thanked you for it later.

## IT'S A MARATHON, NOT A SPRINT

I don't know about you, but I'm not much of a runner. I wasn't very good at sprinting or jogging; it just wasn't my thing. But if I had to pick one or the other, I'd have to say I would have probably leaned more toward the marathon side of things, which is perfect because that's exactly the skill you need as a parent. You've had moments where things were going exactly as planned, on pace if you will. And then there were times where you might not have taken a drink of water when you probably should have, so now you're struggling to get to the next water station. You're not quite sure you'll make it, and you almost didn't, but you kept pressing forward and believing and then, like magic, you were there. You got through a difficult time when it felt like you wouldn't. You rallied your troops when you needed them. You got advice, input, support, and wisdom from your family, friends, or professionals when you really needed it. And now you're here. Still standing and ready for the next chapter, and I, for one, am so fucking happy for you! Because like I said earlier, parenting is not for the faint of heart, which means you're a warrior!

> Now is the time to really begin to pay attention, to start asking the tough questions about sex, drugs, and bullying.

And I'm totally with you. I feel your struggles, and I celebrate your victories. Parenting has to be the most bittersweet experience one can ever have . . . or maybe it's just me. Maybe it's because I didn't have it on my heart to do it that I feel like the accomplishment of raising awesome humans is so monumental? I don't know. But what I do know is that getting your kid into full-time school and tying their shoes on their own isn't where it ends. It's sort of just the beginning. Now is not the time to relax into them being "bigger/independent." Now is the time to really begin to pay attention, to start asking the tough questions about sex, drugs, and bullying. I want to encourage and inspire you to never be the parent with the rose-colored glasses. You know that parent, right? That one parent who confidently and boldly claims: "*Not my kids*, they would never . . ." Don't be that naïve. Be the parent who is able to consider, "Hey, my kid *could* be the class bully" or "My kid *could* have weed in their dresser." Whatever you don't want to believe your kid "might" be doing, check anyway. I mean, what's the worst that can happen? You could be wrong, and they'll probably be offended for five minutes, but trust me—deep down inside they will feel safe in knowing that even though they aren't a "baby" anymore, they're still your "baby" and that you'll stop at nothing to fight for them and their well-being and safety.

If you've practiced balance in your parenting, then you enter these tween and teen years knowing that no matter what storms come your way, you have the solid foundation of love and respect to weather them all. You trust them and they trust you. You respect them, they respect you, and as long as that is the cornerstone of your relationship with one another, you can't and won't go wrong. But believe me when I say that to get to this point in the relationship with this "new person" living under your roof, you must be consistent in your house rules. You must make sure that when the going gets tough, you don't crumble under the hours of silent treatment or the glaring across the dinner table or the refusal to even come out of their room. There will be a whole slew of new attitudes you're going to need to adjust to and learn to take in stride. You may feel like your house is a land mine, and you have no idea what you are walking into every single day. The biggest thing I can tell you about being the parent of a tween/teen is that it's not you, it's them. The sooner you can embrace the fact that they're transitioning from your baby into their very own human and give them the space to do it (and respectfully toward you, obviously), the sooner the battle of strong wills will come to an end in your home.

I mean, put yourself back in their shoes for a moment. Remember how bizarre it was to no longer feel like yourself? To come to realize that the things that used to make you laugh until your stomach hurt no longer cause the same joyful reaction? Do you recall how hair sprouted out of everywhere, your chest started to feel like somebody stuffed a softball under your skin, and your knees ached? You kissed your best friend and you liked it, but you also kissed a boy while playing Spin the Bottle and you liked that too? For boys, your voice cracked and erections happened with a stiff breeze?

It's all tough, and I know you remember how tough it was. For some kids, these moments are when eating disorders present themselves and bullying begins in earnest.

So, be ready. Be ready with open arms. Be ready with a straight line drawn in the sand. Be ready with an escape route for them when they just need a break. But most of all, be ready with the understanding that this turmoil isn't about you.

It is about them.

They need you to be kind. They need you to be firm, but gentle.

They need to know that the awkward person they are transforming into is as loved as the little kid you posted one zillion photos and videos of on your social media. They need to know that as they work this out, as they figure out what the actual fuck is going on inside their minds and bodies, that Mommy and Daddy are still the same. They may be in chaos, they are ships out on a stormy sea, and you are their safe harbor. You must promise me to put yourself aside. Remember how I talked about the key to being an awesome parent is by being a humble parent? Well, this is your time to shine. This is your time to make a vow, out loud, that if you've been harping on them, or overwhelming them with stress and pressure by asking them, "What happened to my baby?" then this is the day that you put all that aside.

Quit it now.

Like now.

I still hear you . . .

You don't do that anymore. You are there to steer, listen, and love. Because this is not about you, this is about them. Love them through these tumultuous days because, my friends, getting your baby from ten to eighteen with all of you intact is a marathon, not a sprint.

So, now that you know this info, put down this book and go have sex with your hot, still-in-the-race-with-you partner. And if you're really not in the mood because, let's be honest, dealing with a preteen/tween/teen is emotionally draining, draw a bath, climb in it with your partner, and catch up on your day. You need that unity and partnership to fight on! And if you're going through this parenting journey on your own, close your bedroom door, slide into bed, masturbate, have a glass of wine, watch whatever TV show you want to, read books . . . do anything that works to connect you back to yourself and happiness!

## Things to Nibble On

♡ So, you had an easygoing, pleasant kid, but now the tween years have hit, and you no longer recognize the child standing in front of you. What's a parent to do? Remember that Rome wasn't built in a day, so get support if you feel out of your league with this new Linda Blair living in your home. You're going to keep your cool anyway.

♡ By laying a solid foundation, you can relax and trust the work you've put in and the relationship you built so you can lay down new rules with confidence.

♡ Just because all their friends are allowed to do something doesn't mean you need to give into their pressure to stand down on your house rules. Also–and none of us like to think this way or tackle it head on–don't be naïve about your kid. They could be a bully, they may be the school asshole, they may be using drugs. Ask the tough questions.

♡ Let's not forget, my friends, that this parenting thing is a marathon, not a sprint. In being the parent of a tween/teen, you must remember: It's not you, it's them.

♡ And definitely make sure you're reconnecting with your partner in a way that feels good to both of you, and if for you that's a good ol' shag, then get to it! HAVE SEX!

*Chapter Two*

# THE ALIEN IN YOUR HOUSE

Alright, I think it's fair to say that we can both agree that the reason you're reading this book is because you now have an alien living in your house. You may even go so far as to say that you have an asshole living in your house. And I feel you on that; I certainly have felt like that a time or two, or a thousand! To add salt to the wound, it feels like it happened right before your eyes. One night you were reading bedtime stories, and the next thing you knew, your kid wanted to tuck themselves into bed, didn't want you to brush their hair 100 times, and didn't need you to give them their nightly bath. They started hanging out in their bedroom alone before and after dinner, and they decided to sleep with their door closed.

Just like that, their childhood years were all said and done.

I totally remember these times in my mom journey. As each of my three girls "transitioned," it was always a surprise, even though I knew it was coming. I have to admit, it always hurt the first time I would say, "What should we read tonight?" and I'd get the "Oh, I'm fine, Mom, I'm just going to chill out." Or when they didn't want me to give them tubs anymore. I have to say that it sort of felt like being "mean-girled" by my own kids. It took me back to those shitty days in high school when one minute you're sitting at a table with your friends eating lunch, and the next day those same friends won't sit with you . . . you know those days; I'm sure you can recall the feeling.

Parenting a tween can throw you off balance and cause you to start questioning where you went wrong. Suddenly you're asking yourself, "How did I fuck up so badly? Things were going so well. Or were they?" Doubt begins to creep in, and you find yourself staring in the mirror wondering what you did/said to make them hate you.

Oh, not you?

Wow. If this is not your situation, then lucky you, you must have sons. No, I'm joking. I don't know one thing about how boys transition from little boys to teens. I do have two brothers, but to be honest with you, I wasn't really paying close attention to them. I know they got up to stuff I would assume all boys do. Some fights. Some breaking of curfew. A little bit of mouthing off. But, in general, not a whole lot of drama. So, whether you have a boy or girl in your house and don't find yourself in this boat during the tween or early teen years, then I envy you. I went through it with every one of my three daughters. And I'd love to say it was smooth sailing every time, but that would be a lie. Sometimes it was a fleeting moment of them rolling their eyes, or it was only one night of no story time and then another week of nightly hanging out together before bed. Just in the way that you are unique, each of your kids will also be different in how they transform from school-aged child to adolescent. (I don't know your life, or your history with your kid, so I can't say for sure that you were on the right track. I can't say whether you were addicted to your phone, thus causing your child to feel as if they didn't matter or you weren't available to them. I mean, I'm not judging, and I'm not saying your kid withdrawing from you at this point in time is your fault, I'm just suggesting that you may be wondering if it was you, and this is normal.)

My girls still bust me for being on my phone too much, and they are adult women. It turns out that our kids don't like it very much, no matter their age, when they deem that we're on our phones too frequently. But challenge them for being on their phones a lot, and I'm talking that it's gotten to the point that their phone looks like a part of their hand and you don't recall the last time you saw them without their device, and what can I say? Welcome to the age of parenting a hypocrite—they now challenge you for the things they actually do, and you choose to bite your tongue because you know that they're closer to having children of their own than they were ten years ago and vengeance will be yours once they have those children, and that day will be sweet because it will make up for feeling like you didn't do a great job!

Because show me a parent who doesn't question what their role may have been when things start to get weird with their child, and I'll show you a narcissist who probably shouldn't be a parent. Questioning yourself reveals the depth of love you have for your kid. It also shows that you care about the well-being of your child and your relationship with them, which is a good thing. Wanting to do more, do better, and be closer to your kid is a healthy response to this new family dynamic you're trying to navigate.

> There are no perfect parents, in the same way there are no perfect children.

My husband says I have a long way of telling a very short story. So, let me cut to the chase: Whatever sort of parent you were up to this point cannot be changed or undone. But I can promise you, and I would bet my last dollar on it, that even if you were the "perfect" parent—whatever the hell that is—and your kid hasn't talked back, has never broken curfew, and wouldn't say "shit" even if their mouth were full of it, even if they haven't done these things YET doesn't mean they NEVER WILL.

I've known tons of parents like this, and I can assure you that these "perfect" parents don't get their kids to their high school graduation unscathed either. There are no perfect parents, in the same way there are no perfect children. The sooner you let go of the pressure of perfection you've placed on yourself thanks to the picture-perfect worlds of Instagram and Pinterest, the sooner you will be free to have an organic and real relationship with your child. Consider this question: Does following "picture-perfect" Insta-parents, who you probably don't even know, make you feel uplifted/supported/inspired/loved, or do they make you feel like you're failing at your parenting game? If it's the latter, then adjust who you follow, like yesterday. We become who and what we surround ourselves with, including our own social media feeds. How can we expect our children to stop the comparison and perfectionist game if we aren't willing to have an organic, heartfelt, real relationship with ourselves and our kids? Besides, isn't this the type of

> The only thing that exists with certainty is doing your best.

relationship you're actually after? Not some bullshit filtered relationship with the person you created, but a real one? One with depth, trust, and authenticity?

I'm going to get real with you right here, right now. I happen to feel incredibly strongly about the fact that social media has caused a great many people to have a warped sense of reality about the world around them. We only used to be able to compare ourselves to our neighbors who were in our direct community—the size of their home, the grades their kids got, who the parent of the captain of the football team was, whose husband had the better paying job, whose wife made the best damn meals and appetizers, which parent was more involved in the PTA, etc. It was a small social circle, but now with all the social platforms out there, it's easy to see in every single minute of every waking hour just how short of the mark you and your kids fall. It is, as one of my staff members is famous for saying, "a literal nightmare" for those of us sensitive creatures who naturally struggle with feeling like we're behind in life to be reminded on a millisecond-to-millisecond basis, "Hey, you! Yes, you! You're failing in this area of your life too!"

Uh . . . no. No, thank you.

I am so grateful that all the social media "norms" were not around when I was fumbling my way through being a mom. Maybe you're not fumbling, and I don't want to put that on you. Perhaps you've always wanted to be a parent and knew exactly what you would do as one—you had the structure all plotted out, and you had your rules and deal-breakers all clearly mapped. I love that, and I truly raise my hat to you. But for those who are feeling a tad wobbly with how things are going and where you're at with your teens, it's important that you remember that the lion's share of what you are seeing on social media is not reality. There is no perfection in life, and there certainly isn't in raising a fellow human. The only thing that exists with certainty is doing your best. The only person you have to answer to at the end of the day is you. Parenting is a rich, fulfilling experience and not one for the faint of heart. However, if you commit wholeheartedly to your role, and if you are willing to be humble, to poke fun from time to time, and to laugh at yourself while crying in your wine glass, you're going to be okay.

I promise. And I can promise because I ended up being okay, and so did my girls.

By now I'm confident that you know you're not alone—that every single parent who has gone before you has not only been in your shoes but has also had to navigate having their sweet, lovely, easygoing child become possessed by, well, I'm not going to say the "devil," but if you do, I won't argue with you. And if your parent partnership has dissolved, hopefully you have your own parent, a sister, a sister-in-law, or a best friend you can lean on when the going gets tough and who can take your kid off your hands when you need to just catch your breath.

If you're extremely lucky, you're a parent who is not yet living in that shit show of a game show, WHO WILL TAKE OVER MY TEEN TODAY?

"Bradley, I'll take Satan for $1,000."

Or you may be fortunate enough to already be deep into the teen years and have not had a single issue between you and your kid. To that I say I'm not only envious, but I'd love to get your number and learn how the hell you did it! But don't get too comfortable; even if you did get one over the threshold with both of you still intact, it doesn't mean that you'll have the same luck again as they grow from teens into adulthood. Lord knows that I didn't with my three, as each one was their own adventure in parenting.

## NO TWO KIDS ARE ALIKE

Not any one kid is alike; my three couldn't have been more different. It was totally bizarre to me that although the house rules were exactly the same for each of them, how they operated within those house rules was completely unique to them and their personalities. For example, our eldest had this thing with changing her hair color, and I don't mean going from her ashy blonde to a beach-girl blonde, I mean wanting it pink and then wanting it blue. She didn't want subtle changes, she wanted BOLD changes. She was thirteen, and every day it was a battle of "Can I now? Please, can I?" Fortunately, our girls attended a school that didn't allow the dying of one's hair, so deciding what to do with this free-spirited, artistic child of ours was deferred until summer break, which gave Yannick and me the opportunity to discuss whether it would be a yes or no from us.

Our middle girl, however, loved being the only brown-haired girl in our family, and she didn't even start to change her hair color until she was in her twenties. There was never a debate with her about why she couldn't have rainbow-colored hair, which was cool since we had a whole list of other things we were trying to get her on side with that we never had to do with our eldest. And then there was our youngest. She loved her "storybook hair" and wouldn't have dreamed of changing it until post-puberty happened and high school proved that the strawberry blonde it had turned one winter was not simply her "winter" hair color anymore—it was her color to stay. And so began her journey of changing her hair color.

What about how your teen wants to dress? Do they dress too provocatively for their age? Does your son want to wear clothes that he's worn every day for the past week? Or maybe he's meticulous, but your daughter wants to wear the leggings she wore to bed to school, then back home, then back to bed again and now they stand up on their own? Or perhaps your son wants to wear skirts and eyeshadow, and your daughter wants to wear blazers and dress shoes?

I honestly don't know what will happen when your kid crosses from young kid to adolescent, and nor do you unless you have a crystal ball, but one thing is certain—it won't be how you expected them to change. And it can be tough on both child and parent as you begin to lose control. You may find that you had a kid who lived for their sport of choice but now you can't get them out of bed on time for their activity, and once you do, you are greeted with the grumpiest little asshole you've encountered since your own "just leave me sleeping" days. Hell, if you're like me, you're *still* a bear to get out of bed at any time of the day.

No matter what crossroad you are at with your teen, it's nothing that a whole lot of love, patience, and firmness won't get you through. Something Yannick and I developed with our girls when they started to become their own people with their own style ideas, their own sassy attitudes, and their own interests was this: If we were going to tell them that they couldn't dye their hair or they couldn't quit all their activities at once, we had to give them three good, fair, sound reasons as to why we were opposing them. But the older they got, the more these conversations turned into what felt like a championship match at Wimbledon. Sometimes it was downright exhausting, and we would wave the white flag. "What the hell. Who cares if she dies her hair pink, then blue, then back to blonde all in the same week? I'm too exhausted arguing with her to even remember why I don't want her to do it in the first place! Do you remember why we said no? Do you even really care? 'Cause I don't care . . ."

And truth be told, there were times I wanted to stuff one of their dirty socks in their mouths to get them to stop asking for the hundredth time why they couldn't have a boyfriend at twelve or thirteen, or why we didn't want them hanging out with that kid who already skipped school (who, by the way, was seen vaping outside the school grounds). Some days you're going to want to just throw your hands up in the air and let them work out their own shit, but you can't. You must not collapse now. Now is precisely the time that you need to remind them that you have these rules for their own good, and you tell them, like your parents most likely said to you, "I say no because I love you." I can assure you that they won't simply melt into a puddle of joy and gratitude, overcome with emotion that you love them SO MUCH. In fact, what your declaration will most likely do is cause them to . . .

**Talk back at you like you didn't give them life.**

Yannick always found the "talking back" part of the girls becoming their own people more difficult than I did, perhaps because I'm the mom and women tend to talk things out, or as Yannick likes to say, "Talk things to death." Or maybe, just maybe, I gave my girls way more grace on the talking back thing because I remembered just how mouthy I had been, so to me, our girls weren't actually *all that bad*. No lie—the number of times I came "this close" to getting my mouth washed out with soap (back when that was a thing that parents threatened, and some may have even done) is too many to recall. In our house, as it may be in yours as well, we found ourselves changing position all the time. Sometimes it was Yannick who blew up at their mouthiness, and other times I was the parent who lost her cool and saw red when they got mouthy toward me. It's hard to remember which of us was sterner on the entire talking back piece of the girls finding their voices, but I do remember that it happened a lot and got handled right

> We directed our daughters to train themselves to handle conflict like an adult.

away. We weren't big fans of having our kids scream at us. Or flip out, cuss, name-call, or throw fits. We just didn't see the use in allowing them to lose their goddamn minds with us over their emotions getting out of hand. So, we would rein them in. We would quickly address the behavior, remind them that it was a completely unacceptable way to handle conflict or upset, and we encouraged them, sometimes gently, sometimes with threat of consequence, to find their respect for us, or their sister(s), super quick. We directed them to train themselves to handle conflict like an adult, even when they weren't one, because ultimately, that's what we are all trying to create. An adult. Not a bully. Not somebody who believes if they scream the longest and the loudest, then they'll get their way. You want to raise a human being who keeps their cool in every setting and knows how to manage their disappointment and their differences of opinion with their emotions in check. After all, feelings and emotions pass, but call a teacher or your boss a bitch, and you'll be dealing with the consequences of that reaction for much longer than you had the feelings.

Am I right?

We know I am.

You see, it's one thing for your kids to have their emotions, their opinions, their anger, their upset, and their hurt feelings, all of which are good, healthy, normal pieces of being human beings. What's not okay is living with a rage monster who feels it's completely fine and justifiable to lash out and dump their shit all over everybody around them. It's just not okay. And if you're a parent who believes that this behavior *is* okay in your house, I will ask you one question: Have you ever seen a work colleague behave this way in a staff meeting and thought, *This is such an awesome way to handle this really tense situation?*

No, you haven't.

Most adults don't behave in this manner. It is not how your kid is going to go out in the world and "win friends and influence people," so don't let them grow up to believe that it is an acceptable way to fight it out at home. Thankfully, our girls were quick learners (or maybe I thought they were, but they were secretly muttering under their breath—kids love to do that!). I recall one time when I was at that age and had a boyfriend. I was a "wise woman" and wanted to go hang out with him on a school night, probably to have sex. My mom was a good parent and said that I could not sashay my young ass over to his place. So, naturally, I responded like any level-headed, respectful teen and said in what I thought was my inside voice, "She's such an ugly pig."

No sooner were the words off the tip of my tongue than my younger brother ratted me out in cold blood. Mouth agape, blonde curls bouncing in shock, he screamed, "MOM! SHANTELLE JUST CALLED YOU AN UGLY PIG!" He barely got the words all the way out of his mouth when I heard my mother roar, "Oh, don't worry, James, I heard her!" What happened after is a mystery because I think I blacked out in fear to protect myself from what I was sure was imminent death.

So, maybe you're *that kid*, one like me who was *soooooooo cool*, feared nothing, and just let your mouth run. I mean, just because we like to express ourselves doesn't make it wrong, right? Ah, no. Wrong. Dead wrong. It's so not the way to handle things or behave. The only person who was able to teach me how to be a decent, think-before-I-speak human was my husband.

True fact.

Perhaps you weren't like me at all. Perhaps you were a great, easygoing kid who was an upstanding, respectful, easy-to-parent teen. Whatever way you rolled as a kid, chances are that you will get one just like you, so if you were an easy one, lucky you. And then you'll get one you have no idea how to navigate or parent because that is how the world works—it constantly pushes our comfort zones, especially in parenting.

One of the parenting areas I never had an issue with my girls about was them wanting to know the *why* or the *how come* of the "Why can't I hang out with them?" When they did ask, I found it was a great opportunity to express the reasoning behind my decision while also teaching them about the bigger-picture life, which is a large part of being a parent. Parenting is not just about saying yes/no to questions they have or to how they want to behave, dress, or live, it's about explaining to them the potential flip side to a choice they make today that may come back and haunt them, not necessarily this week or next month, but certainly in the future should they just jump off the emotional cliff they're currently standing on without checking the depth of the water below them.

Keep in mind that talking things out with them and helping them see the other side of the choice they're hell-bent on making does not mean swaying them over to your way of thinking or being. Not at all. It's about teaching them to make well-rounded decisions, and not just about the color of their hair, but when picking which courses to take and those people with whom to associate. It's about helping them train their minds to take a moment to think through their feelings and not simply react to one because it feels so good in the immediate moment.

Teaching them to think about the big picture comes in super handy when they're offered drugs or booze for the first (or hundredth) time or are pressured to skip class; it comes in super handy when they're under the gun and trying to decide if it's better to be "cool" or to be sober and safe. It is our job as parents to get them discussing *why* "the why" exists in the first place. Get them using their own brain and its ability to analyze a situation and make the best long-term conclusion for themselves. And should they, like our eldest, dye their hair pink and then turquoise all in a short span of time? Guess what? The hair gets damaged and needs to be cut short, but then it grows back. And that's the lesson to be learned about letting go of control. Once you've said your piece and given them your parenting wisdom, if they choose to go in their direction on a subject, then you step back and let them see that choice through. But you must make sure that you're there to catch them if they fall and, for the love of God, don't be the parent on the high horse, wagging your finger and telling them, "I told you so." That's shitty. You know it's shitty because whenever anybody has done it to you, you felt pretty terrible.

Let's agree as adults here that parenting our teen is a lot like treating them the way we want to be treated and speaking to them in the way we want to be spoken to. Lead by example. Keep your cool (or, at the very least, come back to it quickly!), and they'll keep theirs. There is a massive difference between setting up a standard of communication

Lead by example.

♡

you're willing to accept from your teen and controlling them or stifling their free expression. These are not one and the same, folks, so don't get it twisted. Allowing your kid to disagree with you by calling you names or telling you to fuck off is not freedom of expression. That is disrespect, and you need to nip that in the bud right away. Teach them how to argue their point and get their ideas across in a mature, kind, and respectful manner and chances are they will get their way more often because a rationally behaved person evokes confidence in just about anybody. So, teach them to be strong, clear, level-headed communicators by not freaking out when they're freaking out.

I realize that what I'm advising will be hard, which I know from experience. When any one of my girls was giving me sass, attitude, and all the bitchiness of five menstruating women, I didn't always handle it calmly or patiently. Oh, man, did them sassing me bring back memories of me being mouthy toward my own mom. By the way, Mom, I know I've said it many times before, but I'm sorry for how difficult I was as a teen. And you were right—I did get one just like me, and now I totally know what it was like to walk in your shoes!

When my girls sassed me, I often snapped right back at them, and I can tell you that it was when I didn't keep my cool with them that discussions became full-on battles that turned into wars. Nobody wants a war in their home, so learn from my mistakes and keep calm, even when dealing with the most irrational, stubborn, pigheaded, pain-in-the-neck child. And if you simply cannot, if you know you're going to blow up, excuse yourself from the situation (something I failed at time and again, but I did get right every once in a while!). Basically, if you can't keep your cool, then it's your duty to put yourself in a time-out until you can come back composed, parenting from your logical brain and not your emotions. I rarely kept my cool, so my husband often had to put me in a time-out. I actually find it amazing that any of my kids still love me and that Yannick still loves me. I truly figured I would have driven them all to madness by now.

One instance of my many moments of losing my cool comes to mind vividly. During a particular perimenopausal dinner adventure out, something somebody said set me off, and I jumped out of a moving, albeit extremely slow-moving car thanks to a snowstorm (wine and hormones do not go together for me, so it's only tequila now), and our logical and eldest girl, Brianna, took the brunt of getting me back in the car. I love you, Bee. I'm still sorry for that terrible night and my brutal behavior. Oh, did I mention it was the night of our middle daughter's birthday celebration? Some celebration that was! UGH. The mom life is tough. Anyway, all this to say that it is easier said than done, as you can see from my aforementioned confession. I didn't always keep my cool with my girls, and we still love each other and hang out. So, don't get down on yourself if you find that you're unable to do it the first few or 630 times that your once lovely and gentle child tells you to shut up for asking them to put away their dishes.

I know, it's completely irrational, and super weird, right? Get used to it because this is how out of left field, bizarre, and nonsensical you may find your interactions with your teen are from hour to hour. "Hey, will you please put your dirty lunch dishes in the dishwasher before you go back to your room to spend another one hundred hours playing video games?"

"Ugh, shut up, Mom."

Yes, it happens this way sometimes, and you may get the urge to grab that cute little cherub by the back of their neck and say in your best Dwayne Johnson voice, "ARE YOU TALKING TO *ME*?"

But you won't do that, will you?

> Your kid respecting you is nonnegotiable.
>
> ♡

No, of course you won't.

You will take a deep breath (or twenty) and say, "Hey, I'd really appreciate if you would please put your lunch dishes in the dishwasher." And you will stay cool, even if you have to ask ten more times.

Okay, that's a lie. You won't ever ask ten times. You will only ask twice, and if they are still being sassy, then you will give them a choice: They can either put their dishes away or spend one hour without their device. I don't really care which device, but one of them. They need to understand that even though they're all "grown up," they still need to listen to and respect you. You are their parent, after all, and them respecting you is nonnegotiable.

Let me share a little tip. If you take a trip down memory lane to when you were a teen and not listening to your parents, you knew that it wasn't because you didn't trust them or didn't believe they had your best interests at heart. I mean, deep down we all knew these to be true, but when we were in the middle of our teendom, we didn't listen to them because we thought they didn't "understand us" and they were "geriatric and uncool," so like how could they possibly know how we felt?

Remember thinking about your parents in that way? Yes, I know you do. Now, look at your teen and believe that when they're not listening to you, when they're fighting you on a rule you've laid down or when you're asking them to be respectful citizens of the family home/space and pick up after themselves, that their rudeness is not their right to free expression, it is them making a choice to be disrespectful. And call me crazy, but I'm sure your parents didn't tolerate your disrespect, so I would suggest that you not accept your own kid's disrespect. It doesn't need to end in a bloodbath or an autocratic takedown. It can simply be you saying, "I would truly appreciate if you would please do things the first time that I ask you to do them. I don't want to nag you because I respect you too much to do that. I'm asking that you respect me enough to listen the first time." There doesn't need to be any "because I said so" language or raised voices or flared tempers. You can clearly communicate your expectations without losing your cool. And if you're having trouble getting your teen to be respectful, turn it around. I used to say to my girls, "How would you feel if you asked me to do something for you and I ignored you? What would that feel like? Does that feel respectful, kind, and loving?"

Let them sit with that for a few minutes. Walk away and give them space for it to sink in. It may take an hour, a day, or a week, but it DOES sink in. It always sinks in. As humans, we don't enjoy knowing that we've intentionally hurt somebody, especially somebody we love. So, if you are able to call your child back to themselves and put them in touch with their own feelings, or how they would feel if we didn't honor or listen to them when they requested something of us, chances are you are going to win the war and your kid will put those dishes in the dishwasher or wash them themselves. And when they do, my friends, grab your partner's hand and go do something—just the two of you! You've won yet another battle and are now negotiating peace treaties with your teens in their teendom.

## Things to Nibble On

♡ Remember that you were young once too, and it was fun to express yourself through what you wore and what color you dyed your hair. These are not huge sticking points, and I wouldn't get hung up on them. I mean, as long as what they're doing isn't hurting themselves or anybody else, leave them to it. Choose your battles wisely, save your energy for the wars, and try not to sweat the small stuff.

♡ It's super important to teach your child to decipher between an emotional, impulsive decision to do or say something and the ability to see both sides of an idea bouncing around in their heads. It is our job as parents to help them learn to wait on some urges to see if they still feel as passionately about them in a day, a week, or a month as when they first thought of them.

♡ Self-expression and talking back disrespectfully are not at all the same thing. Learn to tell the difference and make sure your teen knows what this difference is as well.

♡ Raising a teen is the perfect time to have blow-off-some-steam sex. So, go get some!

*Chapter Three*

# HOUSE RULES AND THE IMPORTANCE OF FOLLOW-THROUGH

So, we've come to terms with the fact that your kid is going to give you sass and that talking back is just a part of the rite of passage into teendom. You are prepared for it, and you have some tools for how to handle this new version of your precious child whose eyes used to light up every morning when you walked in the room to wake them. If you're lucky, your teen doesn't have an iPhone waking them up, and you still get to enjoy that morning ritual, except for on weekends. Spoiler alert: Teens are like gremlins on weekends—don't get them wet, and NEVER wake them before noon. Hell, I'm fifty-two and I can't stand waking up any way except naturally. But let's be honest: How many of us get to wake up at our leisure? Life doesn't work that way, but wouldn't it be pretty fucking cool if it did?

Or is it just me, a nighthawk, talking?

Alright, carrying on. We've established that your kid will be weird, different, and a bit all over the place. And trust me when I tell you that it really has nothing to do with you and everything to do with them, which means not taking their behavior personally and then mean-girling them when they behave like an alien. Instead, you are going to put yourself in their shoes and parent them through the behavior rather than react to it. You will respond to them calmly and rationally instead of reacting all guns blazing, Incredible Hulk-style.

We also established that your kid is not you. They are their own person, with their own personality, and they will be different than you were in many ways. Know that as long as they aren't harming themselves or anybody else, you are going to relax a little bit and allow them some freedom to develop and grow into their own living, breathing, independent self, not a mere extension of you. Parenting isn't about the resurrection of your unmet needs or unfulfilled dreams and desires being brought to life through your kids. Nope. Parenting is about you helping your teens become *their* best version of themselves. It is about helping them acknowledge feelings as just that—feelings, not fact. You are going to help them find and establish healthy ways of working through the hard, gunky part of transitioning from a child into a teen, with lots of extra love, patience, and humor. Teach them to find the humor in the awkwardness of their evolution.

And then move along. Which is what we're going to do now.

There is a very good reason why this chapter is near the beginning of the book, and that's because it was one of the areas my husband and I fought over *a lot*. We sometimes fought about it in private and sometimes out in the open in front of the girls. It's safe to assume that you, like me, have probably fought with your partner in front of your kids a time or two (or FIVE THOUSAND) as well. Establishing rules for teens is a parenting role that has always amazed me, and truth be told, it is probably the one area I notice the biggest discrepancy in what parents think and how they behave. And this discrepancy starts when kids are young. A perfect place to witness it is on the playground: Some parents sit with their coffee in one hand and their smart device in the other, doing nothing while little Johnny is wreaking havoc and ripping toys out of other kids' hands, simply because he wants them. And Johnny's parent doesn't even look up from their device. Unfortunately, this sort of checked-out parenting continues into the teen years. You will hear it one trillion times from your kid: "Well, Laura is allowed to sleep over at her boyfriend's house," and you will respond as your parents did with you, "I couldn't care less what Laura's parents let her do, Laura isn't my daughter, you are. And you are not allowed to sleep over at your boyfriend's house." Whatever your teen's sexual orientation, they're going to want to have "sleepovers" long before they should, and you're going to have decide if it is important to you. And once you decide if it matters to you, and whether your answer is a no or a yes, then you have to get the other parent on your side so you present a united front to the enemy, who in this case is your kid. Rules must be decided upon together by both parents.

If you're still in a relationship with your teen's other parent, it will most likely be easier to come to terms than if you aren't. Now, notice that I said it will be "easier" to come to terms, and I didn't use language like "it will be a total breeze" or "it will be a walk in the park" to come to an agreement on the house rules with your partner simply because you're together. I didn't use those phrases because I can assure you that when it came to what the girls were allowed or not allowed to do, my ideas often differed from my husband's. I was more often on the opposite side of the yes, sure, why not, they can do that, than not. And maybe it's because Yannick was raised by super open-minded,

Landmark Forum/EST-trained "woo-hoo" type folks who thought nothing of letting a fifteen-year-old reside in a major metropolis alone, in the basement of some friends they knew. So, he did that, and, well, he's still alive so you know he didn't understand why I thought it was wild that our daughter wanted to go on a road trip for two weeks to another province at age thirteen with a family we'd never met. And then there's me. I was raised by a single mom who was raised by immigrants who didn't allow her out past the streetlights coming on and definitely didn't allow her to hang out with boys because, you know, they're bad and you can get pregnant (although they never told her *how* one gets pregnant, and back then neither did schools, so voilà, she found out at sixteen that the way you get pregnant is by having sex).

So, yeah, Yannick and I came from two totally different backgrounds, so we had to find our middle ground as parents. We had to decide what things were absolutes, what things he had to firm up on, and what issues I had to loosen up on. It wasn't easy, it took a lot of time, and it took a lot of conversation and occasional battles, but we got there eventually, and our kids knew not to fuck with us and that we were absolutely 100,000 percent unified on the house-rule thing. So, they didn't. At least not very often. I'd be lying if I told you that they not once ever tried to bend or get around the rules, and that is no way to start our new friendship. I mean, I'm supposed to be the friend who tells you the truth, the whole truth, and nothing but the truth. I'll leave that gala-level surface BS to the girls you used to think were your friends but who didn't tell you about all the stuff I'm about to prepare you for in this book!

The bottom line is that when you're entering the teen years with your kid, you need to have your house rules on lock, and your kid needs to know that these rules are nonnegotiables. I'm not talking about whether they can have chips and soda for dinner while playing another fifty-four hours of Fortnite. No. The rules that you and your parenting partner are going to decide on right here, right now, as in the second you finish reading this chapter, begin tomorrow. And you have to be united on them. There can be no tiptoeing around them. There can't be a divided front where one of you thinks a rule is important but the other doesn't. Once you've come to

Rules must be decided upon together by both parents.

terms on what you both think are the most important things you want your child to abide by, then you call a family meeting and let them in on the new house rules and when they take effect. And in my experience during my thirty-two years of parenting, it's best to make the changes swiftly. Rip that bandage right off, then give them a grape freezie to numb the pain. Don't say, "Well, on the fifteenth day of the seventh month, these rules will start to be punishable." This shit needs to change right away, or your sweet, perfect kiddo will push that envelope one more time. The likelihood of that happening is 100 percent.

Trust me.

## GETTING ON THE SAME TEAM AS YOUR PARTNER

Friends, listen to me. If you haven't already formed a parenting team with your significant other, which (and this is not a judgment but more of an observation) if you haven't, I honestly don't know how you could have come this far. But that's none of my business. The fact that you're here reading this book now and getting organized with your parenting is all that really matters. So, if you haven't already formed a team, now is the time to have a meeting with your kid's other parent. The agenda of this meeting is to establish house rules with your tween/teen. You both must be wholeheartedly on side with the rules that you're going to be presenting to your child, because if you're not, and trust me when I tell you this, kids can smell dissent a mile away. They can read the vibes of their parents like the alphabet—easily. They will instinctively know which one is the weak parent on which rule, so it is key to be unified. The most important thing that needs to happen here is that you and your parenting sidekick present a united front as well as BE one.

"Well, how do we do this, Shantelle, if I think it's super important that homework is done before my kid is allowed to play video games, and meanwhile, their dad/mom thinks they should be allowed to blow off steam for an hour or so when they get home, since they've just finished a day of learning? How do I tackle this issue, Ms. Know-It-All?"

I'm very glad you asked. When our girls were little, we had three house rules (because you don't need to have a whiteboard of rules for them to follow). You want to keep it simple to help make following the rules a part of their character instead of them just doing lip service in front of your face to avoid a consequence. You want your kids to follow the rules because you're

> Good parenting is all about consistency and balance.

♡

consistent and fair and not because they feel oppressed and like they're living in an autocratic hell. You're going to hear me say the following in my interviews about parenting, in my podcast about it, and in this book: Good parenting is all about consistency and balance. So, when you sit down with your partner to devise your family's house rules, you're going to base them on these three check points:

**1) Is this rule we're going to implement an exercise of my authority over them, or is it in their best interest?** That best interest can be in regard to their safety and their quality of life and be relative to their maturity.

**2) Am I creating this rule because it makes my job easier? Or does it have a real bearing on making a difference in their life as to the aforementioned reasons why I would create a rule?**

**3) Is this rule necessary and fair, or is it a holdover from my own childhood?** For many of us, when we set about establishing a rule in our own household, it's often simply because it's how we were raised, and we haven't really explored whether that same way of being is relevant and necessary for our own mini-me running around, which is precisely why only you and your partner can determine what rules need to be set in place. If you're finding that you cannot come to an agreement about what rules to establish, then I suggest that you seek outside input. Find a couple's therapist (if you don't already have one) who can help you come to understand the other's point of view. For example, I survived a rape at a young age, a sexual assault from a family member, and an attempted rape from a group of boys I went to school with, so I am hypervigilant in protecting my girls from assault. For me, an extremely important rule that I needed Yannick on board with was that our girls were not allowed to sleep over at somebody's home that we had not been to with them, nor were they allowed to sleep over at a friend's house if we hadn't met the parents. We had to know the parents and have a vibe about them. It was then, and only then, that they were allowed to sleep over. My husband didn't fight me on this rule because he was empathetic to my past/reality. He respected my history and honored it by agreeing with me on this rule. But there were other rules I wanted to put into place (because I'm a type A personality and a natural worrywart) that he had to stand firm on and declare "ridiculous" and "excessive."

It was a dance to get to the rules that we felt were key to their safety and to their development as human beings. And when we couldn't agree, when we were at an impasse, we would turn to our unbiased third person to weigh in and help guide us. And if you live in a separate household from your teen's other parent, I respect how much more difficult it might be to arrive at a mutual ground of agreement on the things you want your teen to adhere to, and often, if your kid is like 99 percent of the rest of the kids on this planet, they will play both ends to the middle for their own gain. Thus, when you're running a kid between two households, it's even more important that you be unified, because—and this is me speaking from experience—there's nothing a kid loves more than to know that at Dad's place they have no curfew, while at Mom's, they can't be out on a school night at all, never mind until midnight! So, let me be clear here: There is nothing more important when parenting a teen than exemplifying the importance of unity between their parents, and this applies to whether you live under the same roof or not.

Now, if you find yourself in a scenario where your ex is still living in their anger over the dissolution of the relationship and there's no speaking reason to them, then I suggest that you have a frank sit-down with your teen and have a clear, mature, and honest dialogue as to what the house rules are in YOUR home. Provide them with the reasons why you have made these rules and what the "code of conduct" is while they're at your home, as it were. If you're struggling with finding the words to explain to them why there are different rules between the two households, I encourage you to speak without attacking or ragging on the other parent. Now is not the time for your kid to learn that their parent was a chronic adulterer or that they never wanted kids and that's why the marriage didn't last.

Okay, I may be exaggerating here, but you get my point. Now is not the time to label them as the loser parent and that the reason *you* have rules for your kid is because *you* actually care about them . . . this is not the time to do that. This is the time to speak matter-of-factly: "This is my house, I love you, and I feel very strongly that a, b, and c are all important rules because they result in x, y, and z, all of which are what's best for you." Speak openly and honestly with your teen and chances are, even though they might not like your rules or agree with them, they will at the very least respect you and where you're coming from. And don't worry, they'll figure out their own work-arounds in time.

I kid, I kid. Your teen will totally and absolutely respect your house rules and never break them, not even once.

## CONSEQUENCES, AND WHAT THEY SHOULD BE

Okay, a bit of sarcasm, but it leads us beautifully to the next topic in this chapter. Your kid is going to break the rules. It is a given. So, now that we know they will, we need to come up with a plan for what happens when your mini-adult is disrespectful or abusive toward you. What is your reaction? What is the consequence when they blatantly give you the middle finger?

I don't know your specific setup or the character of your children. You might have one stubborn and bold kid on your hands who fears nothing: not you, not losing access to their devices for a year, nothing. Like nothing can get this kid to "play by the rules." I had one this way, as did my own mom . . . you're bound to have at least one, especially if you have a household with multiple kids in it. Since we're new friends, and I'm not yet privy to your kid's attitude, I can't tell you what consequences to put in place to aid in getting your teen to think twice before stealing from a store or your alcohol cabinet. Only you know what your offspring values more than breaking the house rules. So, once you have that on lock, then you'll know what punishment fits the crime. When they're little, it's easy to take away their favorite book or toy for a few hours. When they get older, however, it's much more complicated because their worlds have expanded, which keeps you on your toes. Do I tell them they can't have sleepovers for a month? Do I take away their smartphone for a day? Do I keep them from their extracurricular activities for the week? What do I take away to get them to understand that I mean what I say and say what I mean?

The key to getting your teen to follow the rules you've established is to make sure that when they break one the first time that the consequence is significant enough that it makes them seriously reconsider the next time they want to disobey the rules. And the other way to ensure your teen "gets it" depends on your follow-through. You must follow through. No ifs, ands, or buts. And this, my friends, is often the hardest part of parenting your teen. You must have the stomach to put up with the bullshit that's going to come your way when you do take away their gaming privileges or their device. They are going to flip out, so be ready for it, and don't break. Follow through.

May the force be with you, right?!

And for those of you who are shaking your heads right now and saying, "This is so wrong. Kids need to be free to learn from their own mistakes. We can't squash their individuality in this way. You're too autocratic, Shantelle," think of this:

*Am I?*

*Am I really now?*

Let me ask you a few questions:

Do you drive on the right side of the road when you get in your car to go somewhere? Do you take off your shoes at airport security when asked? Do you stand in line at the grocery store to pay for items instead of just taking them?

I'd be willing to bet my last dollar on the fact that you answered yes to every single one of these questions.

Sure, they're silly.

Sure, they're obvious.

Sure, every person answers yes to these questions, because *everybody does them.*

Okay. Fair enough. These were way too simple do-you-or-don't-you scenarios, so let me ask some not-so-obvious questions.

When writing a test, do you cheat? Do you troll and bully people online?

Maybe you have done these things, and it may be because you don't think they're so bad, or perhaps it's because only you know that you're behaving badly in these areas. These rules and guidelines aren't as obvious and are more of a moral-compass–type thing, unlike the out-in-the-open societal rule breaking, as it were. And our kids may think, "Well, breaking that rule is not that big of a deal because honestly, who am I hurting? It's not like I'm killing somebody." And while they may have a point, it is our job to teach them that there are checks and balances we are accountable for in every area of our lives. Sure, we can have our opinions; we can storm the Capitol if we like. We can bully people online or lie to our teacher or tell them to kiss our asses if we don't like a grade we receive. But the reality is, no matter our reaction to the "rules" that are laid out before us, the consequences still exist, whether we like them or not. Whether we choose to follow the rules or break them, the way the world at large works, for better or for worse, is that for every action, there is an equal and opposite reaction. This is fact. This isn't open for negotiation. This is the world you are sending your teen out into eventually, so whether you agree with how the world operates or not, you need to prepare your kid to be accountable for their actions and the consequences that result from them. Do yourself and your child a favor: Set them up for success in the *real* world and help them understand that they can choose to behave however their heart desires, but the reality of their choices will not be left unchecked. You're not doing them any favors by allowing them to believe otherwise. And if you don't teach them this reality in the safety of their own home, I have news for you—they will learn it in university and beyond at the hands of strangers, peers, professors, and bosses. Somebody will

> It is our job to teach our kids that there are checks and balances we are accountable for in every area of our lives.

eventually teach them how the world works, and it most likely won't happen kindly or through love, so wouldn't you rather it be you?

## SINCE WHEN DID DISCIPLINE BECOME A DIRTY WORD?

I am fascinated by the parents who have decided that their child should never hear the word "no" or that their kid can push somebody else's precious child off a jungle gym and not get in trouble for it because, you know, that's just "Timmy being Timmy."

No, it's not, Karen. That's Timmy being a fucking bully, and you need to get that shit in hand, like yesterday. For real. Healthy, well-adjusted kids don't behave like that. Trust me. A kid hurting other kids at will is not how all kids behave, at all.

It equally amazes me when I hear parents proudly declare that they've never disciplined their child. I mean, I've had three. Did you know that? Did you know that I have three adults that I birthed and raised? Ugh, I feel like I say it a lot when I write my parenting books, and it gets on my nerves a little bit because by now you totally know that I have three humans that I grew and raised. But I say it because my kids were totally different from one another, and I had to discipline every single one of them, and often. I mean, it was either that I disciplined them or one of us was getting locked in a room for the rest of their days, and that's not practical, or legal. Instead, I opted to discipline them so that they would grow into people I truly admired, loved, and thoroughly enjoyed. I'm of the opinion that if you want to send your child out into the world capable of withstanding any challenge that comes their way, then you parent/train them in the way the world really works. Set your kid up for victory, not failure. You won't be there to catch them when they miss a deadline on a paper at university because they were happier playing video games day in, day out instead of doing the assignment. You won't be there when they get cut from the team because they didn't practice during the off-season when they should have. If you want them to succeed in this one life, then you must raise them to be prepared for it. Like fully and wholly prepared for it. I'm not claiming that you can predict what's going to come their way, but what you can predict is whether you help them develop the sort of character that can handle even the shittiest parts of life. We don't have to like it when life is hard, unfair, cruel, and awful. But we must be able to withstand it. We must be equipped to ride the highs and lows with the grace and faith that it will all be okay in the end. We must empower our kids to accept the difficult times as gracefully as the good times.

There are two prominent, trendy parenting styles right now, and the parents who follow them often practice them well into their children's teen years. You might recognize yourself in one of them. If you do, it's not too late to flip it on its head. Many of today's parenting methods have a short-game mentality.

**Helicopter parenting** involves "hovering" over your kid. By not allowing your child to learn about life through their own organic experience of it, you are stealing from them. When you do everything for your child, you're literally taking away all the exploration of self-discovery and their ability to use their own brain for problem-solving. You're not always going to be around, so make sure you give your child what they need to succeed, and a big part of that is trusting in their own ability to get to the other side of a problem by finding the solution themselves. Think back to your childhood: Would you have liked it if your parents buffered everything that you had the opportunity to learn on your own? Figuring shit out by yourself is empowering! It makes your kid feel like a superhuman. Coddling breeds insecurity; it tells them that you know they can't do something on their own and that's why you *must* do it for them.

Not cool.

Next up we have the **lawnmower parent**. The lawnmower parent constantly buffers life for their child so that everything is smooth sailing. This parent "mows" difficulties out of their kid's life, clearing the way of all hardships. Like helicopter parenting, this parenting style is not going to create strong, resilient adults. Your kid may feel better in the moment because of your safety net there to catch them or because they never face struggle, but I'm writing this book to give you a *long-game* mentality.

> Set your kid up for victory, not failure.

You want to make strong, secure humans, so you all will have fuller, richer lives. Parenting, my friends, is about balance. Don't take any shortcuts. Discipline your kids. Be consistent, fair, and organized. In other words, have house rules. In our house, the "line" was clear, and everybody knew what the punishment was if someone decided to cross it. If you discipline this way, you will have a home with much less drama in it. I know; I created one.

There are some parents who feel as though discipline, structure, and rules cause their teen to conform—that their teen won't have the freedom to evolve into their own person or have their own thoughts, feelings, and freedoms. I say, how about we change the perspective on this belief for five minutes? Hear me out.

Why not?

Alright. So raise your hand if you have a friend who has never talked about their admiration for a championship athlete. Anyone? Anyone at all know somebody who doesn't have mad respect for a gold medal Olympian? Raise your hand if you have a friend who has never claimed that they want their kid to be good at the so-and-so sport they play. I mean, come on. We all know somebody who wishes their kid played well enough to be a professional athlete. The Olympics or champion series of any sport gets tens of millions of viewers. And why is that?

Well, let me answer that for you. It's because we're in awe of their fortitude of character. We deeply respect the level of commitment and hard work that it took to get them to the top of their game. We RESPECT IT. Yet somehow, we're happy to raise our own personal noodles. We love people who have the character to become a champion, yet some of us don't want to instill those same values into our own kids. So, let me ask you this: How do you think that my friend Tessa Virtue, the most decorated figure skater on the planet, became who she is? Or the hockey team that wins the Stanley Cup? How did Kobe, Michael, and LeBron become the best of the best in the NBA? How do you make a champion? Well, I'm going to tell you. You make a champion by telling them that their last effort wasn't "good enough." You make them do that floor routine "one more time" until it's good enough to win a gold medal. Parents, listen to me when I tell you that champions are not born, they are MADE. You become the best when you are challenged to aim higher. You become a champion by being trained and by being asked to give your all, every time. You must not settle for minimal effort; you must do better than your personal best. Now, I know you may be thinking right now, "Calm down, Shantelle, I'm not raising an Olympic athlete. I'm just raising my kid."

Fair enough. I didn't raise any Olympians either, but what I did raise was kids who have the character of a champion. I always expected them to tell me the truth when I asked them a question, and you should expect the same from your kid. I let them know that I would never tolerate throwing a fit as a way to deflect them from having to do what I asked. I also parented them in a way that made it very clear that if they wanted anything from me, they couldn't be sly or manipulative. Instead, they had to come right out and ask me. They needed to communicate clearly, respectfully, and intelligently if they hoped to get a yes out of me.

It's actually pretty wild that we admire the win at any cost in our athletes, but for some reason, we're soft on our kids. We don't want to be "too hard on them," but we also want them to achieve the same things that these athletes do. What? How is that going to happen? It doesn't make sense to me—it never has and never will. I mean, you have one life, and you only have one chance to raise your kid, so why not raise a champion? Now, I'm not telling you that you can't think your kid is the absolute greatest fucking kid that ever existed whether or not they end up being a pro-athlete, Olympian, or couch potato. I have three, and trust me when I say that they did and do drive me crazy, but even still, I want the best this life has to offer for them. I fully believe that my girls are the smartest, most wonderful, amazing people I know, but that doesn't stop me from calling them on their bullshit—even though they're grown-ass women at thirty-two, thirty, and twenty-four. I don't let them off the hook when they're being assholes, even now. But here's the beautiful thing: They don't let me off the hook when I'm being an asshole, either. And that's totally fine and cool because they trust me and know that I'm their biggest fan, and I trust them and know that they think I'm pretty okay too. So, how about you just relax and enjoy your kid? I mean, it's totally okay that they're not likely to be number one in their class or captain of whatever it is they're into. Not everybody ends up in these top spots in life, and the reality is that most of us land right in the middle. Not a single one of my daughters was a captain of any team, nor were they members of Mensa, but you know what? It didn't make a damn bit of difference because I still loved them with my whole heart! Nothing made me love my three incredible girls any less, and nothing will make you love your kid any less, either.

It's pretty straightforward, and I think I presented a pretty sound and reasonable case behind the necessity for rules, boundaries, consequences, and discipline if you want to raise a fully functioning member of society who can hold their own and is equipped to not only get through life but *thrive* through it. And that means you now have this all sorted. You and your co-parent are on the same page, and you've established rules and consequences that you both agree are worth enforcing. Life is good! And I know that you're feeling like a massive weight has been lifted off your shoulders, which brings me to my next suggestion. What can you do with all your freed-up energy?

Read that book!

Take that hike, or that weekend retreat to pamper yourself.

Find a lover, if you're single.

Reconnect with your partner, if you've got one, and spend time getting intimate. And if your intimacy leads to sex, well, you know how I feel about that . . . HAVE SEX!

*Things to Nibble On*

♡ You've realized, whether you and your teen's co-parent reside under one roof or not, it is time to establish some rules for this next stage of life. Keep them simple and try to stick to rules that will ultimately make your teen an excellent global citizen, not just ones that make your family bubble run smoother. Think bigger-picture character traits you want to instill in them and about rules that keep them safe.

♡ Whether we like it or not, or believe there is a utopian way to live life, the real world works on the principle of "for every action, there is an equal and opposite reaction." Newton said it, not me, so don't shoot the messenger. Keep this fact in mind when parenting your teen. You must prepare them as best you can for success outside of your four walls, which means that there must be consequences for when they don't do as they're asked or when they break one of your rules. Be reasonable, and make sure that the punishment fits the crime. There is no need to go crazy here . . . keep your cool.

♡ We all love professional athletes and rock stars and somehow want our kids to achieve this same level of success without the need for discipline. It can't happen. If you want to raise a champion, then you have to do so with structure and discipline. It's the only way.

♡ Now that you've done this work, you've got an abundance of time to use as you like! So, it's time for all that juicy self-care goodness. Start that new hobby! Take that trip! Build a deeper bond with your partner! Make sure you keep your other relationships a priority, the one you have with yourself and the one you have with your partner. And don't forget to fit in SEX!

*Chapter Four*

# FRIEND OR FOE AND HOW TO HELP THEM TELL THE DIFFERENCE

We're moving right along! Don't you love how straightforward this book is? It's not like you need a PhD to figure out what the hell I'm talking about. Perhaps a lot of what we're chatting about here you are already implementing, or maybe my parenting tips were already on your radar but you thought you'd be the "too strict" or "too tough" parent with your rules, so you didn't implement them. Perhaps you haven't pulled the trigger, as it were, and not because it's not how you desire to parent your teen but rather it has more to do with the fact that you might be saving face with other parents, or you know you've allowed your kid to think they're in charge up until this point and you're really too exhausted to turn this ship around now, thanks in large part to having lived in a pandemic for more than a year. Here's the deal when it comes to saving face with other parents or when you're a finger's push off the cliff from pandemic-parenting exhaustion: You are *you*, and your kids are *your* kids. Only you know instinctively how to best protect them, love on them, guide them, and help them thrive. So, how about we make a pact? You promise to trust yourself more when it comes to parenting your kids. And how about only taking advice from people who are raising or have raised their kids in a way that you admire and appreciate? Start as you intend to go. Don't pull back on the rulebook or on the tough conversations with your teens. They may not appreciate it in the moment, but a decade down the road, and even when they are much older, they'll appreciate all the ways in which you helped them thrive.

There can be a mountain of reasons why you haven't yet implemented house rules, or why you haven't established consequences for your kid's poor behavior and choices, or why you thought discipline was a dirty word. I hope that since we've covered these topics in the last chapter, you've changed your mind. And let me tell you this little bit of info: Many parents have written to me since I wrote my parenting book on kids, saying that they are thankful that I spoke about all the things I did in that book because they felt that way too, but they thought they were all alone in how firm they wanted to be with their children. Reading my book helped them feel connected and supported in their instincts to ask and expect more of their children. It is my hope that you, too, will feel that way as you move through this book with me. I told you at the very beginning that I'm a really good friend, and as you can see, I really am!

Let's keep keeping on.

This chapter is so important. I don't know about you, but my experience with friends while I was growing up was touch and go. There were many times I thought I had a ride-or-die friendship with somebody, only to learn later that it was one of those "friend for a reason, a season" type of relationships. I had to work really hard at gleaning the value of the friendship, extracting the good stuff while simultaneously mourning it. Then there were the times when a person was around just for what they could get out of their friendship with me—purely transactional—and those were the ones that stung the most. I have to be brutally honest with you: I am a very good friend, and when I don't get that same loyalty reciprocated, I lose my mind. I take it really hard, like curl-up-in-the-fetal-position-for-a-day (or two or twelve) type of hard. Now that I'm fifty-two, it's not so, so bad, but I still have to really work through the loss of a friendship. I'm sure you have countless stories of the ebb and flow of your own relationships and that you can call up the heartbreak of the special and important ones coming to an end, either dramatically or organically just fading out. Whatever your experience with the relationships in your life, if you're the kind of parent I am, you don't want your kids to suffer one bit at the hands of another human being. You want them to make friends easily, and for life. You want them to be treated with respect and love. You want to know when you should step in and help them navigate the waters, when you need to step back and let them come to you, or (and this is the hardest one of all) when to just keep your mouth shut. Let your kids figure it out. Let them work it out and determine the ones worth fighting for, and the ones who are not.

It is tricky, let me tell you. I have on many occasions stepped in and gotten involved when I shouldn't have or said too much about a friend or a lover when I totally should have stayed silent. In reality, my kids were just trying to blow off steam and gripe about them; they didn't really want me to tell them what I thought of their friend or lover. But I thought they were done with that relationship, that the nail was in that relationship coffin. And boy, oh boy, do I regret that, because then we'd fight and they'd inevitably yell, "YOU DON'T EVEN LIKE SO-AND-SO AND THEY'RE WAY NICER TO ME THAN YOU ARE!" or some version of that, which I'm sure you did as well when you were their age. I know I did.

I'm going to help you learn to tell the difference, understand the hidden messages, and decipher the secret signals they're sending you, because I do believe that I've finally unlocked the code of HOW to help them navigate a rough patch in a relationship.

FINALLY!

I'm also going to help you decipher if/when your teen is being an asshole to somebody else's kid. Often, our kids are so good at playing us and presenting to us their best/perfect self that we can miss the signals of them being little tyrants out in the world. In this chapter, I give you some things to look out for and tell you how to uncover who your kids are when you're not looking. And since my goal with this book is to ensure you're raising the best person YOU can raise, I'm going to begin by focusing on you and your teen first. It's like I told the mom who wrote me a note, ragging on my kid while her girls were being the original Girls Gone Wild, "Tend to your own garden."

So, this is where we begin.

## DEDUCING IF YOUR TEEN IS A GOOD FRIEND OR NOT

Figuring out if your kid is a good friend or not can be tough. A surefire way to tell is by considering how long their relationships last. I mean, if they have a revolving door of friends, then chances are they're not the sort of person who people enjoy being friends with, for long. Maybe they're too domineering, or maybe they don't know how to be authentic in their friendships. There can be a whole gamut of reasons why they don't have any long-term relationships, and it may not be very easy to uncover, mostly because teens are pretty good at keeping their emotions close to the vest, and often it's because they don't know how to articulate everything they're feeling. I mean, hell, I'm a full-grown adult and I have a difficult time expressing myself wholly and clearly some days, so imagine how much more difficult it is for our teens.

If you're noticing that your teen doesn't seem to maintain any long-term friendships, it's time to start paying attention to the patterns you see happening. You might be wondering, what do I mean by patterns? Since you're not at school with them and you're not on their phones reading their social exchanges, how are you going to be in the loop of potential patterns that are sabotaging their friendships? Well, I said it a lot in my other book, and I'll say it in this book too: As a parent, it's totally cool for you to think that your child is the bee's knees, that they would never be a bully, an asshole, a know-it-all, or an introverted, insecure, timid human out in the world. But if you think back to your own teen years, there's probably a chance that you were all these things as you were learning to become a full-fledged adult. I know I embodied all these character traits throughout my journey of trying to figure out who I was. So, let's agree that we're going to love our teen, respect them, think the best of them, and be their greatest fan while also being open to the possibility that they might be struggling with any number of traits that can hinder them from establishing and nurturing healthy relationships outside your family circle.

The main role in your job as a parent is to keep your mind open to the possibility that your kid isn't perfect and to be okay with that. Coming from this place of acceptance allows you to recognize that your teen may be the problem in their relationships. And once you determine if they are in fact their own worst enemy, you can help them pivot.

There were times when I was a shitty, shitty friend. Man, the stories I have. For starters, in my younger years, I couldn't keep a secret if my life depended on it. My mother used to say there were three ways to send a message:

1) telephone
2) telegram
3) tele-Shantelle

And you know what? I'm not even mad about her saying it. I knew she was speaking the truth. But if I wanted to have friends, I had to quit that behavior right away. I also had to stop wanting to win all the time, and I had to stop being bossy. Not everything could go my way. I couldn't always be Sandy when we played *Grease* (Penny, you were so

> Do your kid a favor and teach them how to be a good friend.

gracious and allowed me to be Sandy EVERY TIME!), and I couldn't always hold the microphone when we performed our family concerts. I had to learn to share, and I had to learn how to be a good friend, and the best way I learned to be a good friend was at the hands of other kids pointing out what an asshole I was. So, if you're too busy to teach your kid how to be a good friend, you don't really have to sweat it, as the other kids will do it for them. But speaking from experience, it's way better if you help your kid get there. At least you'll do it from a place of love and not with your fists in a dark ravine. Yeah, that did happen. I did get beat up in a ravine by a pack of girls who heard that I had called one of them a name . . . so do your kid a favor and teach them how to be a good friend.

Alright, now back to the point. Patterns of behavior. So, what patterns are you looking for? For starters, listen to how they speak about their friends. And when they're on phone calls, or when they have friends over, listen to *HOW* they speak to them. Are they respectful? Do they use a demeaning tone or language? Do they run the show? Are they inflexible in planning? Do they name-call? If you're actively listening, you'll find out pretty quickly what sort of friend they are. We've had name-calling kids come through our house, and if I'm being totally honest with you, because that is what best friends do, I've heard my girls be the berating asshole too! Yes, it does happen. Your kid will dish it out, so don't be surprised to learn this fact about your precious child.

I'm all for a little bit of cheek and sass, but you can tell the difference between your kid "joking" around with name-calling and being verbally abusive. If it is the latter, well, my friend, you need to step in. Your teen may think they are being funny, or that their friend knows that they're "totally joking," or state that "she talks to me that way too, so relax." No. Don't fall for it. You know that old saying, "Sticks and stones may break my bones, but names will never hurt me?" It's bullshit. Pure and utter bullshit. I mean, I don't know about you, but for me, when girls in my high school wrote SLUT on my locker in lipstick, that shit stung. I cried. It hurt. A lot. And I remember it like it was yesterday.

So, parents, please do the world a favor and don't allow your kid to run their mouths about anybody, and especially not the people they say are their best friends. Name-calling isn't funny, and name-calling hurts. Period.

I also encourage you to really listen to what your kid tells you about their friendships in the event that you have straight-up asked them if they are a good friend and it hasn't resulted in an open dialogue with the truth rolling right off their tongue. When they're in conflict with a friend, have you noticed that it's always the other person's fault? Is everybody else stupid or an asshole? Is everybody in their circle mean to them? Do they claim to be left out or use victim-like language?

I used to say to our girls when they complained about the same issues that were showing up in all their relationships over and over again, "What is the common denominator in all these friendships?" They'd look at me blankly, and when they ultimately shrugged their shoulders, I would casually respond, "YOU."

This answer allowed them to stop and take stock in what patterns they were repeating again and again, and it was one of the most helpful lessons I taught them to do in their relationships. They needed to stop the tape recorder they had playing in their minds about what they perceived their friends *were doing to them* and look at what they were doing consistently in their relationships that was causing them to break down.

The key to uncovering what sort of global citizen your child is, is to read between the lines with them. Pay attention to what they're telling you by talking super casually about their own life while driving back and forth to school, over dinner, or whenever or however you glean your knowledge. You will learn so much about your child if you are fully present when they're speaking around/to you. And if you've determined that they are not, in fact, a very good friend, then it's time to get to the root of why not. What is it about their personality that keeps them from treating people in the way they want to be treated? Is it because they've been spoiled? Did you "my precious child" the shit out of them? Is it because they never learned to lose or had to come to the very real, yet healthy realization that they're not the best, brightest, most talented kid in the room? Is it because, like me, they had so much trauma while growing up that the bravado and the bossiness were just cover-ups for insecurity? Or is it, like it is in one of my girls, just in them—just the way God made them?

Whatever the reason your teen may not be a very good friend, it's never too late to point out to them that life is long and filled with many different people and varying personalities. And the best way to succeed and soar in life is to become the sort of adult who can be respectful of these differences in others, be a person who treats *everyone* they encounter—not just the people in life who are "like them"—with the same respect with which they want to be treated. The first thing that comes to mind about kindness and equality is in respect to other's sexuality. When I was growing up, we knew nothing about LGBTQ+. I mean, as far as I knew, I had never met a gay person. I did kiss my best girlfriend a lot when I was little and liked it, but I also kissed boys while playing Spin the Bottle and liked that too. I mean, it's kissing, and kissing is awesome, and fun, and, well, sexy and grown up! So, for me, when I was growing up, there wasn't a lot of talk about anybody not being heterosexual, probably because it wasn't really a time when people could freely be who they really were. Now, as an adult looking back, I do recognize that some kids in my school were very clearly homosexual, and I hope with my whole heart that they are now living happy, full lives married to someone they love. Because that would be a beautiful thing. Your teen has definitely met other teens who are already out, or who are struggling to find the strength to come out. You may even have a child of your own who is gay or who doesn't identify with the gender they were assigned at birth. I don't know. But what I do know is that we live in a time where it has become a little bit safer for them to live the life they want to lead, at least for the most part, though prejudice and discrimination still take place and not everyone feels free to be who they really are. And that breaks my heart. Why can't people just be who they are and love who they love? It's beyond me how the way somebody chooses to identify affects anybody else's life. I truly don't understand why it would matter to anybody at all, or where this intolerance resides.

But let's not dwell on that! Let's instead lean into the future and celebrate knowing that there are a great many places on our big, beautiful earth where kids, and maybe your own kid, can be true to who they really are and love who they really love. And don't underestimate the power of raising people who are this way. Accepting. Honoring of others. It is your job to raise the little humans in your household to be tolerant, to be decent, to be kind. It doesn't cost them, or any of us, one thing to be kind. If somebody ends up not being for you, then you walk away from the relationship. If your kid doesn't understand how their friend who used to be John is now Julia, that's okay. They don't have to relate. They don't have to understand. The only thing they have to do is accept, and without judgment. It's that simple. Be the parent who raises a person to not only behave with respect but be someone who believes that mistreating somebody, or bullying, or being unkind isn't okay. And listen—if you happen to discover that your kid is the problem in the group or is intolerant of how a person identifies or of who a person loves, then I urge you to be the voice of reason that draws them back to a center that is rooted in acceptance and kindness. And

> Raise the little humans in your household to be tolerant, to be decent, to be kind.

if you come to learn that it is your kid who is the bully, the one at school who is ostracizing other kids or starting hate campaigns against somebody else's teen, get involved. Early. Nip that right in the bud. Put a stop to that behavior. Don't wait for it to pass or work itself out.

Step up and step in.

## WHEN KIDS DON'T LIKE YOUR KID

This topic breaks my heart so much. If you are a living, breathing human being, you've experienced not belonging. You've wanted to be part of a crowd that hasn't wanted you, like for sure. There is a 1,000,000 percent likelihood that you've experienced being left out, and when you're emotionally vulnerable and twisted up inside, is it not just the absolute WORST? Didn't you want to DIE? Or was that just me?

Well, if it didn't happen to you, I'm deeply and extremely jealous. Lucky you. And just because you may have gotten off scot-free doesn't mean that it's not going to happen to your teen. Chances are it will if it hasn't already. Anyone else watch *Thirteen Reasons Why?* If you haven't watched it, I highly recommend you watch it with your teens so you can have an open, informed, heartfelt conversation about the highlighted topics and behaviors. So, get ready for it.

You know that famous Elizabeth Stone quote? "Making the decision to have a child—it is momentous. It is to decide forever to have your heart go walking around outside your body."[1] It is the absolute truth about being a parent. I don't know if a parent ever arrives at the utopian place where they no longer worry about their children. If you're not worried that they're being bullied, you might be concerned about whether they are the bully. Honestly, there's always something in the back of your head about your kids as they grow into their own people.

It's enough to make you drink . . . actually, it DOES make you drink! Wine, anyone? Or is it too early for a glass of bubbly?

Let's keep on keeping on!

We got lucky with our first girl. She didn't run into too much trouble with kids, and she often ran in a large circle of friends. She was always a pack girl. She played well with others and got along easily with both boys and girls. She was involved in theater groups and choir, was a competitive skater, and did martial arts. She was super busy and social. To call her a strong, grounded, confident kid would be an understatement—she was a force to be reckoned with. And I believe all these strong, positive character traits helped her avoid being at the center of many bullying campaigns. She wasn't the natural pick for mean girls. There was only one traumatic situation. When she was in fifth grade, a half dozen sixth-grade girls decided that they were going to regularly terrorize her. They shoved her in the hallway and called her a slut. She was *ten*! Where did these girls even hear that word or learn that behavior? Then they started to link arms, follow her around, and swarm her on the playground, any chance they got. And why did they do this? Well, for no other reason than good ol' fashioned jealousy. Some of the sixth-grade boys thought my daughter was cute.

And so it begins. The tale as old as time when young females repeat the pattern of relational aggression between females. And the claws come out, pure mean-girl style. *If a boy doesn't like me but likes you, it means if I'm mean to YOU, he will eventually like ME.*

No. Just no. It doesn't work that way.

Parents of girls, I'm with you as a fellow girl mom, and I want to pass something on to you. It's up to us to teach our daughters to respect other people's relationships. If a man is spoken for, dating, engaged, or married, that man is TAKEN, as in off the market, and girls need to respect that and move along and find their own man. If you've ever been cheated on, like EVER, you know firsthand how it fucks with your confidence, your esteem, and your ability to trust moving forward. It's a terrible life experience that none of us would ever have to live through if women didn't have sex with men who are already in a relationship.

Parents, it's up to us to instill character into our daughters. Morals. Infidelity is a line that no female should ever cross, and the only way they will know not to cross that line is if we teach them to just say NO to married/taken men. Tell them often so you don't end up raising a homewrecker. Now, parents, let me be clear: I'm not saying that it is wholly on women to say no; obviously, men need to keep their dicks in their pants. So, can we as parents at least make this commitment to one another that along with raising men with the character to be faithful, let's also raise women who won't be part of the infidelity pool? Let's teach our daughters to be a true champion for other women. Let's teach them the real meaning of "sisterhood," and that starts by never intentionally bringing harm or sadness to another woman.

And if somebody doesn't like you, they don't like you. You can't bully them into liking you. You can't manipulate them into liking you. You move on. And you go and find the person who likes you just the way you are—for YOU. You don't, you know, use your father's gun to shoot up your school because a girl doesn't like you. You don't commit suicide because the entire school believed the rumors spread about you by some bratty, chatty, catty teen who, by the way, is probably dealing with their own emotional and mental turmoil. I'd love to say that these scenarios are a stretch, but sadly, you and I both know that they're not. We've read far too many news stories about a kid who shot up their school because they were not welcomed into a group or weren't loved by someone.

These are definitely the most extreme reactions to social exclusion from peers that a shunned teen might display or act on, and thank God they don't happen as often as they probably could because that would be tragic for so many reasons, and for so many families. You'll never hear me say that I understand why a teen would go to these lengths to express their pain and anguish because I cannot even begin to fathom how violence is their only option for healing or relief. They must experience so much pain and hopelessness to go to these lengths. I'm also not going to say that anybody is justified in turning to violence as a way of solving any issue, but I do often wonder about the parents of the kids who bullied others so mercilessly. How did these parents not know the depth of trauma their kid was inflicting on another teen? Also, how is it that a parent of a child who turns to violence as their solution to a painful problem did not see the signs? I cannot imagine a parent not recognizing how much pain their child is in, or not knowing that they have a propensity to violence, especially if that child has access to an arsenal of weapons and is simultaneously struggling with mental health issues, or depression, or rage.

I wonder these things out loud because I have witnessed cruelty firsthand through my own experience and that of my girls. We've taken cruelty from others, and I'm embarrassed to say, we've dished it out. I'm sure we've all been on both sides of this fence in our lifetimes. We have all had to deal with that kid who was completely heartless, that kid who excluded you or your child for no good reason. The reality with kids is that when they do shun another child, it's rarely done gently or with sensitive and emphatic language. Chances are it will be harsh. It will be unfiltered and presented with little to no consideration.

So, what's a parent to do?

Well, do the best job you can to prepare them for other people's behavior and actions. You explain to them that people can sometimes be extremely mean, thoughtless, and cold, and you educate them to the fact that more often than not it has nothing at all to do with them and everything to do with the aggressor. You tell them that every single time somebody decides to not be a good human, it speaks more to how they were or weren't raised to care about the way they communicate with/ treat others than whether or not your kid "deserved it." Teach your teen that although bullying and exclusion are terribly painful, they are unfortunately not avoidable. But what is avoidable is how they allow that aggressor to affect them emotionally.

Guide. Teach. Build. That is your role as a parent. You are their anchor. These are your cornerstones as a parent, and you must do them consistently so that it becomes second nature to your kid. Make sure it *is in them* so when the time comes for them to be heartbroken, it doesn't lead to violence—against themselves or somebody else. Don't raise them so that these types of emotional letdowns blindside them. Teach them from a young age that they are worthy, they are brilliant, they are lovable, and just because other people don't see that in them doesn't mean that their people aren't out there waiting for them. Give them hope for believing that better relationships are coming their way, and give them the tools to understand that what other people think about them is not truth, it is simply their perspective.

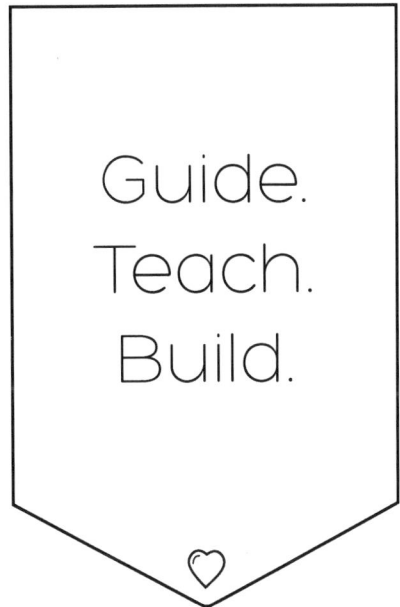

Guide.
Teach.
Build.

Got it?

Good.

Let's go back to that playground situation my eldest girl found herself in all those years ago. These older girls saw nothing wrong with targeting a younger girl. They saw nothing wrong with trying to tear down another girl because they wanted to be cuter, smarter, more popular. This behavior is super dangerous, and parents must not allow their children to get away with it. It is unacceptable and can, and does, cause other people's beloved kids to take their own lives. How your kid treats other human beings is serious business, like the most serious business that you need to tend to as a parent. The way your kid speaks to other kids, the way your kid treats them, the way your kid is when you're not looking is so, so crucial that you must be involved. You must be having regular, honest conversations about who they are when they are not with you. You need to be in communication with their teachers, asking them questions like "Is my kid kind to their fellow classmates?" and "What sort of reputation does my kid have among their peers?"

Be the parent who believes that it could be your kid who is the bully, because I'll tell you what happened with that group of girls. Nothing. We told our daughter to go to her teacher. We initially had her attempt to handle it because we believed that our daughters needed to learn how to fight their own battles in life, that they needed to problem solve and conflict resolve without us being in the middle of it. So, she did. She went to the teacher, but that only escalated their aggressive behavior because then she was a snitch. Great.

Our next piece of advice was to go to the principal. The principal handed it down to the VP, who told our daughter to ignore them and to play on the other side of the playground. And that was that. No meeting with the girls, no conversation, no insistence from a person of authority to stop bullying and terrorizing a younger student. As the bullying escalated, I did what any momma bear would do in this position. After witnessing my strong, vibrant, outgoing daughter cry nonstop, be unable to eat or sleep, and become nauseated at the thought of having to go to school, I went to the school myself. And when the girls came for her, like they did every day, I told them all that if they ever bullied my daughter again, I wouldn't go to the principal, I'd go to the police because what they were doing was harassment.

Was that too much? Maybe, maybe not. But I got what I wanted—they left my girl alone. Finally. But that wasn't the end.

Want to know what happened next?

They told their parents what *I* did, not what *THEY* had been doing for *weeks*. Not what could have possibly led a mother to that breaking point. And you want to know what the school officials did? They called me and my husband into a meeting. Not those kids' parents, not the bullies, but the victim's parents. They chastised us. They told us that the parents, all of them, were insisting on a meeting with us because they wanted an in-person apology from me. And you know what I told the vice principal of the school? I told him that they could all kiss my ass, that it would be a cold day in hell before that ever happened, and if they approached me on their own to try and discuss the situation that I'd press charges against them for harassment too.

And then it finally stopped. Our daughter was never bullied at that school again. But it wasn't the last time my girls were bullied. I could truly write an entire book on how cruel children can be to one another, from both perspectives. Because as you recall, I was bullied, but I also bullied. So, I know what to look for on both sides of this coin, and the reality is this: The best way to uncover what is happening to your child when they're not at home is to ask them what's happening when they're not at home. And if you truly feel like your kid is not giving you the straight goods, then be committed to having an open, honest dialogue with your child's teachers. Be involved. Be present. Be aware. The only way to really know your teen is to be engaged in their lives.

> The only way to really know your teen is to be engaged in their lives.

Now, this engagement may not always be easy. Some teens really don't want their parents "meddling" in their lives. They're reserved, or introverted, and it may be more complicated to get to the root of how life is shaping up for them. If you have a child who is this way, I have found that even with kids like this, they have somebody in your circle they are drawn to, someone with whom they feel most comfortable and free. Bring this person into the loop of what you suspect is happening at school and out in the world for them. Teens have it so hard these days. I mean, holy shit! They're growing up in a time when nothing is secret. If they don't get invited to a party, they instantly know about it because it is splashed all over every form of social media that exists. Back in the day (there I go again, talking like I'm ninety-five instead of fifty-two!), we had to wait until Monday to find out that we'd missed out on a shit-ton of fun over the weekend. But not now. Nowadays, it's in their face 24/7, which is why I'm not a big fan of teens having social media. And yes, I know this is not a thing that can/will happen, but if I had my druthers, and I was raising a teen in today's world, I absolutely would not let them have social media accounts, as the mental illness ramifications are not to be messed with!

Don't believe me? "In the last decade, increasing mental distress and treatment for mental health conditions among youth in North America has paralleled a steep rise in the use of smart phones and social media by children and adolescents."[2] Want to know who made this claim? Researchers from the Hospital for Sick Children in Toronto. And they would know, am I right? And you want to know what they suggest parents do about it? Talk to their kids about the risks and establish rules around social media use.

As I said in my first book, I'd rather be overly cautious and keep my kids protected and healthy than be way too casual with my rules around social media and be wrong. Because when you're talking being wrong about the potential negative side effects of social media on our youth, I dare say the possible negative outcome is too much to lose and, in my opinion, not worth the gamble. But more on social media later.

Whether you like the woman or not, Hillary Clinton had a reason for saying that it takes a village to raise a child, because it does! And now that modern society has us so spread out from one another, where Western culture no longer has us communing with our elders or living in multigenerational homes, the divide and the loneliness for our kids grows larger. Some of them spend more time on their devices than they do with actual people. They need to be cocooned, protected, and cared for, and not to hurt your feelings, but sometimes they don't want you to be the person doing these things for them. I'll be frank with you: There were times in each of my girls' lives when I wasn't that person. Sometimes there were things they felt more comfortable sharing with Yannick, and other times it was an aunt or one of my close friends. As they grew older, they started to share things with one another that I was not, and still am not, privy to. This sharing with others is called "the village," and it is not a time for you to get your feelings hurt—it is the time for you to remember that your teen's emotional well-being and development isn't about you, it's about them. Don't get your nose out of joint if your kid doesn't want to share their most vulnerable thoughts and feelings with you about how life is going for them out in the world, just be thankful that they're willing to talk to somebody about it. Because the reality is that you want your child to learn on their own how to recognize when they need support. You want them to seek guidance when they feel lost and to know that they always have options for getting a helping hand out of any tricky/dark situation they may find themselves in. As their parents, we want to teach them about a variety of methods for handling a bully, or loneliness, or depression, or identity issues. And that might not be you, and you need to be okay with that.

I do have one stipulation for your child seeking the help of others, however, and that is that you make sure they're talking to somebody you approve of and they're not divulging their deepest thoughts/secrets to some online "stranger" or someone with whom you don't have a relationship. You need to establish this criterium with your kid: "Listen, I'm cool with you feeling uncomfortable sharing this stuff with me, and I completely respect that you would rather speak about it with somebody else, but for your safety and my peace of mind, I only ask that it be somebody you know that I trust and who is aligned with what I know is best for you."

Now, just because you ask them to follow this expectation doesn't mean they're going to do it, and this is when parenting your teen gets uncomfortable. Mostly for you. When you ask them to do as you ask and they politely (or not so politely) decline your offer, a shift starts to happen—the shift of letting go. You have to start loosening your grip on them. You need to allow them to test the waters of being grown up by allowing them to make their own choices with the advice you've given them. You can give the advice, but they don't need to take it. It's called free will, and it's pretty shitty when it starts to happen in your relationship with them.

Here's the thing, though.

You may think, "Yeah, right, Shantelle. While they live under my roof, they will do as I say."

Yeah, I thought that too. But the reality is, when you stick your heels in and insist that they do what you want them to do, you're inviting them to go and do what they want to do in that situation behind your back. So, what Yannick and I did, which I think worked out very well, was gave them our opinion on the matter and our recommendation on a course of action and then let them do with it what they would. It sometimes worked out that their course of action was the right one, causing it all to work out beautifully for them. And other times it did not, and we, of course, were there to catch them when they fell. Try it. Let go a little, loosen the reins, trust that you've been doing the work their entire young lives and that they are mature, decent, and thoughtful humans who will land on their feet by making healthy choices. You can trust me on this. Because if there is one thing I've learned through my three decades of parenting it's that your kid will listen to you, accept your advice and lean on you if they know you're sincere. But how, how do I get my teen to heed my words of wisdom? Well, it starts with you being open with them and listening to them, really listening to them. Be vulnerable with them (in an age-appropriate manner, for God's sake!). Teach them by example and you can never go wrong. Walk the walk and talk the talk, and that's how you'll win their respect during the tumultuous teen years.

Teenagers hate a hypocrite but don't mind being one! HAHAHA. I laugh, but it's true.

Now, you might be on the other side of the parenting spectrum in that you have a teen who you cannot, no matter what you do, get out of their shell, to be a joiner, to socialize with even one person. To want to take risks. To get out on the skinny branches of life and try to fly out of the nest. I didn't have a child that was this way. Not one of my girls was shy or kept to herself. They were all fairly gregarious and social. So, for me to sit here and try to guide you through having an introverted kid would be foolish, since I don't have the faintest idea how to navigate the waters of getting a child like this to step into themselves. I do, however, have girlfriends who had children who were deeply and profoundly shy, and they all claimed that the book *Quiet* by Susan Cain helped them learn how to parent this type of child.

From what I've heard, Cain's book is brilliant. It is powerful, insightful, and deeply helpful if you have a quiet kid you may not quite understand. It will open your eyes and educate you. And the truth of the matter is, a lot of what your quiet kid is going through may not be their fault—after all, we do live in a world that truly doesn't know how or when to just shut up! Life is so busy. So loud. Everyone is running from place to place all the time, stimulated at every corner, and they are often overstimulated before the clock strikes noon every day. But rather than me muddying the waters, I'm going to encourage you to research this book and determine whether you feel it will help you. I mean, Cain is a *New York Times* best-selling author, so I'd say you and your kid are in excellent hands with her!

Anyway, the long way around to the bottom line is this: As a parent, we need to impart onto our kids that not everybody is going to like them; they're not always going to make the team, or get invited to the party, or sit at the table with the "cool kids." And all of that is just a normal part of life. We need to teach them how to cope with rejection—from sports teams and from fellow human beings. As long as our kids aren't being abused by somebody, as long as they're not being bullied or targeted by anybody in their peer group, then we must have frank conversations with them about how the world actually works. We must always be thinking, "How do I prepare them for real life? Not the fantasy world I wish we all could reside in, but the real world?" We need to always operate from this mindset. The best way to raise a strong, well-adjusted human is to raise them fully prepared for the way the real world works.

And it is your job to raise a human who links arms with all humankind, not just the ones who look and act like them. Because let's be frank: Everybody being treated equally and justly has no bearing on whether your child can also succeed in life. The quicker we all get on board with this fact, the faster the world becomes a better place for us all to live.

## GETTING YOUR TEEN OUT OF A TOXIC OR ABUSIVE RELATIONSHIP

The first rule for getting your child out of a toxic relationship is to empower them with the knowledge of what a healthy, nurturing relationship looks like, and the first step for imparting this knowledge is probably the most obvious one: have your own healthy, positive, balanced, and nurturing relationships, starting with the sort of relationship you have with yourself. Your children need to witness that the best way to make sure you end up in a good relationship is to make your own self-care a priority. Self-care can present itself in many ways: daily exercise, meditation, journaling, alone time, a night out with friends, a weekend away alone every few months to recharge yourself, bath time for an hour with candles, music, and a closed door. Love yourself first. Care for yourself boldly and loudly so your kids will learn that no matter if somebody else shows up to love them, as long as they have a deep and true love for themselves, then they're already ahead of the game. It's a lot harder to dupe somebody who is switched on and in tune with themselves than somebody who is pining, lost, and searching for love outside of their own self. So, let's start here!

> By watching you navigate your relationships, your kid will learn to imitate you on their own.

The next way to impart the wisdom of how to be in a good, strong, healthy relationship is by having your teen witness how you allow your key friends to treat you, speak to you, keep their word to you, and how you handle it when there is a conflict in those friendships. Are you able to speak frankly and plainly about how something they've done affected you in a hurtful way? Are you able to have conflict and conflict resolution in a friendship and keep the relationship intact and become stronger for it? By watching you navigate your relationships, your kid will learn to imitate you on their own. They're always watching and they're always listening.

You also need to be mindful as to what sort of intimate romantic relationship you're in that they're witnessing, which is an obvious tip, I realize. But as I mentioned, they are watching and listening to everything that goes on around them. So, if you're in a romantic relationship where you allow your partner to break their word to you over and over again, your teen will learn that it's not important if a partner keeps their word to them. If you tell your teen to be kind and respectful to their person yet you yell and demoralize your partner with your language, then they'll never believe a word you tell them about how they should treat people or allow themselves to be treated. And, of course, if you're in a verbally, emotionally, mentally, or physically abusive relationship, I implore you to get help. Somehow. In some way, get out of it for the safety of yourself and the current and future safety of your child(ren), and break that cycle of abuse. And this abuse can be blatant, like being hit regularly, or it can be more insidious with subtle, demeaning actions that torture you on a mental level, so please get the help you need to ensure your kid won't think that it is a normal way to be treated by a person who is supposed to love you most on the planet. Getting help can be as straightforward as calling a local hospital, or women's shelter, or a mental health line. Or it may be as complicated as pulling in a professional to help give you the tools you need to plot your extraction. Wherever you find yourself in your primary intimate relationship, I pray it is in a good place, and if it's not, then I wish you the strength to find your way out.

And if you want a surefire way to teach your kid how to pick a great partner, date your kid.

Yup, I said what I said. Date your kid. Having dates with your kids is an excellent way for them to learn through experience what it means to be truly loved and cherished. It is a natural and fun way for them to learn the difference between a healthy and unhealthy relationship.

Yannick and I learned this strategy in Dr. Mary Pipher's book *Reviving Ophelia*, and we immediately added date nights to our family calendar. She wrote at great length about the importance of having an individual relationship with each of your children, if you have more than one. And dads, I'm watching you. Don't check out right here and now because you think this advice doesn't apply to you since "close friend-type relationships are a mom's job."

Not so fast. According to Dr. Pipher, if you are the proud dad of a daughter, then your relationship with her is actually in many ways much more important to her healthy development than her mom's. The same goes for mothers and sons. Time alone bonding with their mother is a powerful way for sons to learn about and understand love from a woman. Fascinating, isn't it? Once we put this advice into action, "dating" each one of our girls became the most important event on Yannick's calendar every week. It didn't need to be an epic date (those were reserved for me!), but it had to happen. Sometimes it was a bike ride, other times it was going to see a movie, and more often than not, it was just running errands together and getting shit done, side by side, and growing closer with every single date. It was amazing to watch the girls open up thanks to their time with their dad, and let me tell you, it really taught them the level of attentiveness and care they were willing to accept in their dating lives. It was profound and life changing for all of us, and I have to confess that I'm deeply grateful we learned about it while they were young.

Another way we grew their close relationship with their dad was by developing a family tradition when our girls turned ten. Soon after their birthdays, Yannick would take them on a week-long trip to a place of their choice. Now, before you get upset with me and say something like "not everybody can afford that," this trip doesn't need to be extravagant! We're not all Kardashians over here! It can be a camping trip. It can be a road trip to see a cool landmark like the Grand Canyon, while camping along the way. Get creative. Keep an open mind and remember that the key to this double-digit trip is to develop a deeper father-child bond, not to set them up for unrealistic five-star holidays and designer everything! The development of this bond is the primary goal and focus here, not how Instagram-worthy the trip is. Besides, if your kid is ten, they technically shouldn't even be on Instagram . . .

But that's a whole other conversation we'll get to later.

The importance of your kid(s) knowing on a cellular level the distinction of a positive, healthy relationship is paramount. Not every love partner shows their true colors in the beginning of a relationship. I read somewhere, or my girls read it on Bumble or something, that when dating, it takes (on average) four months for people to reveal who they really are. A human can only hide their true nature and tendencies for so long before their true self begins to come out. So, make sure you teach your kid to look for warning signs early on that a person isn't being "authentic."

Often, a relationship starts out beautifully, as if it is "too good to be true." In fact, the person is usually super encouraging to your teen, a champion of theirs, as it were. Your teen's new romantic partner can be their greatest fan, and they may even shower them with verbal adoration and gifts, making it all the more difficult for your teen to notice that the relationship has taken a turn. And it can happen so subtly. For example, their young lover may suddenly just want the two of them to eat lunch together without the rest of their friends. Then they may insist on walking home alone together and hanging out and doing homework with nobody else around. Your teen may have to stay on the phone with them while they walk or drive somewhere. Slowly, this partner is making themselves the center of your teen's world by discreetly stealing all your kid's time and attention, until one day you realize that your kid's friends have stopped coming around, they no longer call, and your teen has become completely dependent on this relationship. Perhaps your teen hasn't realized it, or perhaps they do and they've asked you for help. There are many scenarios as to how a toxic/abusive teen relationship may develop or reveal itself, and my advice to you is to end it immediately when you see it. Get involved, either by bringing in their closest adult relationship to speak with them and uncover the reality and scope of abuse that's taking place or by getting professional help, if needed. I'm a big fan of pulling in experts when I don't have the expertise to help my kid face a particular issue.

Your teen may be fully blind to an abusive relationship, and when that happens, it's scary—I know because I had to stand by and watch it happen within my own household. I'd love to tell you that when you notice something like abuse occurring in their lives that they're responsive and thankful that you love them enough to advise them to get out of it, and they immediately throw their grateful arms around you and tell you that they love you more than anything . . .

Sadly, nope. That's not how it goes down. That's not how my mom responded when her mom told her my dad was no good for her (and newsflash, he wasn't), but like my mom says, "I wouldn't have ended up with my three kids if I had listened to her, and I wouldn't change that for the world." I also did not respond gratefully when my mom told me that my high school boyfriend was a sociopath, or how my girls reacted when I tried to get them out of their own toxic relationships. As a parent, you can tell your kid that you know they are in an unhealthy intimate relationship, and they will flat-out ignore you sometimes. Other times, they will come to you and ask for your help in getting out of it. Nobody can say what's going to come your way when your teen is learning how to have adult relationships, which is what's so dark and scary about parenting teens—the depth of not knowing and how the unknown can have such potentially devastating outcomes on your teen socially, emotionally, and, unfortunately, often physically.

As parents, we know that we went through some not-so-great shit too. Some things were painful while you were growing up, and some experiences, like for me, were downright traumatic, so we know what's out there, and we so badly want to keep our own children from experiencing anything remotely close to our worst situation. So, if your teen finds themselves in a similar experience, I implore you to get help, and get it sooner rather than later. I suggest that you start with contacting a school nurse or guidance counselor—somebody who is where your teen is throughout the day who can check in on them and give them support in breaking free from the relationship.

At the end of the day, you're their parent, and you have to trust your instincts. When your gut is telling you to step in, just step in. Your teen may not like it in the moment, but in the end, they will feel more loved than if you acted like you didn't know what was happening. And if you've done a great job and raised them well and taught them to honor and respect themselves and they still don't listen to you when you express your concerns, then you have to do what I did and wait for them to take the initiative to end the relationship themselves. I realize this advice is not ideal and can lead to many sleepless nights, but the cold, hard truth about raising an adult is that you have to let them fall sometimes, and sometimes they break some bones in the fall, but in the end, they learn. And hopefully, they don't repeat the same mistake twice.

Friendships and intimate relationships aren't the only ones that have the potential to be toxic in your kid's life. You might find yourself in a situation where you're helping your kid navigate an abusive relationship with a teacher—one who is kind, gentle, and supportive of your child to your face but then makes fun of your teen in front of their peers when they get an answer wrong, trying to publicly shame them into being "smarter." I've lived through this experience, as has each of my girls. Yannick's first language is French, and the way he was ridiculed as a kid by some teachers as he struggled to learn English was downright cruel. Now, I'm not bashing teachers here; I happen to think they are all underpaid for doing work I could never do, ever. I didn't even have the patience to homeschool my own children, never mind a whole whack of kids, raised in all sorts of ways by all sorts of people, year after year after year. So, if you're a teacher and an empathetic, patient, and kind one, thank you—this next section isn't about you, or for you, but just like cops, there's always bound to be some assholes in the barrel, and that's who I'm addressing here and whom I'm advising parents to be on the lookout for.

Once you have a teen in high school, I'm a big believer of parents staying the hell out of their school lives, unless your kid wants you involved. But as far as challenging teachers and stepping in, that behavior ended in elementary school, in my opinion. When your teen finds themselves in the middle of a difficult relationship with an authoritative figure, it is a perfect time to teach them how to express themselves in a mature, calm, and educated way. Because let's be honest here: They are going to have to deal with assholes their entire lives because my book on how to raise a good human only came out in 2020, so that's a lot of years when people were raising bullies, assholes, and generally not nice humans! We need to coach our kids how to navigate the world with these people in it, especially when these types of people are in positions of power—the power to give them a good grade or not, or the power to allow them to graduate or not. This shit happens all day long. Not all people become teachers with the best and purist of intentions in their hearts. I mean, I had a teacher in grade four who stood me up in front of my entire class, tightly squeezed my arm, and asked my classmates to say good-bye to me and wish me good luck on my modeling shoot. And no, she didn't do it because she legitimately thought it was cool, she was ridiculing me and making fun of me for being a child model, something I know for a fact because when I had to leave class one time before to go to a shoot, she led me out by my hair while berating me the entire time.

So, you see there are some bad eggs out there who will present one way with you, and a completely different way with your teen. Give your teen the tools to stand up for themselves so they will always be able to walk confidently in the world with the knowledge that being two-faced says more about that person's character than your kid's character. Don't fight the battle for your teen but do give them the weapons so they can fight them on their own.

As we wrap up this chapter, I hope I made one thing clear: The best way to know how your teen is being treated at school, how they feel in their social situation, and whether they're safe in their intimate and closest relationships is for you to be present, involved, and available. Have open, genuine, and loving dialogues with them. We guide, help, and raise awesome teens by being aware and doing the work.

Now, you may not agree with me on this point, and you may likely feel like it is an impossible task, but you know I'm going to tell you to make sure that while you're in the thick of all of this shit with your teen, you're also having sex with your partner. Trust me! Regular sex with my husband was one of the few things I looked forward to while we were in the trenches of raising our teens! And if you're a badass single parent, well, you know what I'm going to say: Get your sexy on yourself!

## Things to Nibble On

♡ Be involved with your teen. Make sure you are listening and paying attention to the sort of friend they are. These are the years when they may begin bullying to save themselves from being bullied. It's a dog-eat-dog world in high school, so be close with your teen and ensure that they're not becoming hardened by other kids to protect themselves.

♡ If you have a teen who is left out for whatever reason, have a village in place to support them through their loneliness. Research how to best support an introverted child through these years so they have recourse for their feelings. Read a lot, help them find activities that build their confidence, and give them purpose and a social group outside of the confines of high school.

♡ Get involved if you notice that your teen is in a toxic relationship, whether it be an intimate one or platonic. It's important to educate your teen on the dangers of staying in it. If your teen is the perpetrator of the abuse, then you must get them help. Don't turn a blind eye if you notice abusive tendencies in your child.

♡ I know you're not going to feel like it, and you're going to think I'm crazy, but keep yourself sane by making sure you take the time to remember that you're a grown-up with needs, so be sure to continue to make time for sex!

# Chapter Five

# LET'S TALK ABOUT SEX

Ooh, baby, here we are. We're at the hot potato chapter. Sex. Would you be surprised if I told you that most adults don't even feel comfortable talking about sex themselves, let alone talking about it with their children? In my book *Raising Your Kids Without Losing Your Cool,* I wrote little reminders with one central theme at the end of every chapter—that couples need to be present in their relationship with one another and be conscious of one super important detail: SEX. Have it. Enjoy it. Prioritize it. Your kids will grow up and go on to lead their own lives. But if you've neglected your intimate relationship with your lover to put your kid(s) first, you might not even make it to this point as a couple. Your partner needs to be the most important relationship you have in your household (other than the one you have with yourself). Trust me when I say your kids need you two to be solid. They want you to be solid! Your relationship being on fire gives your kids a sense of security that nothing else can. Believe me. I've been married to my man for thirty-three years, and we've never been better. But it took us everything we had to get here. Yes, we've had some shit, and yes, we broke up for a year, and we had been prioritizing date nights and sex, and we *still* almost didn't stand up under the strain of life and parent-hood. But we made it back around, and hopefully me writing these books will help you avoid the relationship pitfalls, so you don't have to break up to work out. And one of the ways to ensure you make it lies in having a healthy attitude around sex. Your own as well as your teen's.

## REMOVING SHAME FROM SEX

Let's be completely honest here. Nobody is listening—it's just you and me, two adults being mature about sex. Do you remember when you first felt sexual? Like when you thought, "Wow . . . touching myself there feels really, really good?" And not like the same sort of good as brushing your hair, but like good in your stomach and in your toes? I'm talking *different* good.

You going to be shy here? You don't want to tell me. Alright, I'll go first. I was about eight. I started early, just like my boobs. I had to buy training bras at nine, and I got my first cycle at eleven, so hormonally speaking, I was pretty "advanced," which came with its own set of prob-lems. Older males saw me as an object from a very young age, which I now know has a term: pedophilia. Not okay. And it became a problem.

So, why am I telling you that I started feeling sexual at eight? Is it so you think I was some sort of horny weirdo? No. That is not what I'm trying to accomplish. In fact, I want to stress the fact that sex is, well, natural. And the joy, pleasure, and ecstasy that comes from sex begins at a young age.

When kids are young and "masturbating," it isn't considered "dirty." It's not until a parent has the talk with a kid, usually when it's too late (like around age twelve or older) that they start to dump their shit about sex onto their child. I've sat on panels on national television with parents who are adamant that they will not call a vagina or a penis what they actually are, which is a vagina or a penis. They also don't want the schools to educate their kids on sex.

Come again?

So, you're not going to talk to your kid about sex, and you're pro-testing and campaigning for schools to not be allowed to talk to your kids about sex, so, pray tell me, where will your child learn about sex?

From watching porn on their devices?

From their friends, who probably are learning about sex from porn?

From the internet?

Parents, let's have an open conversation here. If you don't educate your kid, then who do you think should? I mean, truly, who? Because regardless of what you think or believe about sex, it's a natural part of life, and it's out there. Your kid will find out about it eventually, no matter how hard you try to shelter them. So, how do you educate your child about sex if you have shame around the topic due to how you were raised, your cultural beliefs, or other reasons? While I don't know what your personal relationship is with sex, I can only suggest to you that if you have work to do on healing your thoughts about it, please do so. And if you have any negative emotions attached to sex that surface, I encourage you to seek some healing as well. For example, if these emotions influence how you talk about sex with your child—that sex is bad and that your kid is bad and dirty when they have urges—then I strongly recommend that you seek out some healing. Your emotions are valid. I hear you. But it will do everyone in your household a mas-sive favor when you can have open conversations that aren't viewed as "bad," "taboo," or "evil." And this advice is coming from a person who is a survivor of sexual abuse. I have done a lot of healing and can honestly say that I have a strong and healthy relationship with sex, so

I'm confident that you, too, can bring about a change in your negative thoughts and feelings about sex, which you may consciously or unconsciously be passing down to your kid.

## YOU HAVE NO ISSUE WITH SEX, BUT YOU DON'T KNOW WHEN TO TALK TO YOUR KID ABOUT IT

A common question I often get asked is "What age is a good age to tell my kid about sex?"

Well, unfortunately, you're not going to like my answer. If you haven't already openly and honestly talked to your kid about sex and they're already a teen, then YIKES, you're a little behind the eight ball. However, all is not lost, but you have to act fast. Yannick and I have the sort of household where nudity is not a big deal. When our girls were little, we walked around naked after showers and the girls bathed with Yannick. They always knew that daddy had a penis, and they did not. Once they got to be about five, tubs with Daddy stopped, and as they got older, accidentally seeing their dad naked was, well, "disgusting" and "awkward!"

You may not want your kids to ever see their parent of the opposite gender naked. And that's totally cool. You do you. Whatever works for your family is all good, and I completely respect it. But I implore you to not make sex a taboo subject or wait for the "perfect age" to start to talk about it if you want your kids to have a healthy relationship with it. I'm going to go out on a skinny branch here and say that since you're reading my book, you're obviously here because you want to have more open conversations and reduce the hush factor around topics that are related to parenting a teen, such as sex. So, allow me to share with you how we handled it with our girls. You ready?

We told them the truth. Ta-da!

We also told them that it was amazing, fun, and exciting, and it was often the best part of life when things weren't going well. We explained that you can count on sex with your partner to help bring you pleasure and reprieve during the storms of life, and that consensual sex is good sex.

That's pretty much it.

We had open and honest conversations about sex in an age-appropriate way with each of our girls. We didn't make a big deal about it, ever. Not once. We didn't send out a memo alerting them to an open discussion about sex on Monday, January 28, at 5:00 p.m. in the living room. We just talked about it. Nothing formal, nothing heavy, just this: Sex is natural. You may or may not like it one day. You may be really little when you start to masturbate, or you may not like to masturbate at all. You may like kissing and having sex with people who are the same gender as you, or you may like to do it with somebody who is the opposite gender. Only you know, and you'll know when you know.

It was really that straightforward and simple and clear because the reality is, sex is not at all complicated—it is just us and all our own hang-ups about it that make it weird.

True, right?

Yes. Yes, it's true.

So, may I ask you to please do your kids and their future lovers a

> I implore you to not make sex a taboo subject.

favor? Don't let your sexual hang-ups become your children's hang-ups. It's really and truly that easy. It is a choice to be cool when it comes to sex.

Case closed.

## TEACHING CONSENT AND THOUGHTFUL SEXUAL INTERACTIONS

If you're the parent of a son, I want you to pay particularly close attention to this part of the chapter. Now, don't shut down on me. Don't get ready to message me and say, "I am raising a decent man to be respectful of women and to know that *no* means no. Don't come at me about my perfect son. What about the parents of girls? What do you have to say to them?"

First, I want to say calm down. How about you read this section before you get your knickers in a knot? Then, when you're done reading, if you're still all fired up, come at me. I can handle it.

Can we agree?

Thank you.

Here's why I want to primarily address the parents of sons in this chapter: Some of what I'm going to say is based on life experiences, my own and those of many other women on the planet, and then there's statistics, and they don't lie. Well, that depends on who you're asking. It depends on your opinions on fake news, cover-ups, and conspiracies. But for this moment in time, let's agree to believe the statistics. Moms, I want you to think back to when you were a young girl. Who groped you in line at school? Was it another female, or was it a male? When somebody kissed you at a party even though you said, "NO, I don't want you to do that," was it a girl or was it a guy?

When more than one in three females has been sexually assaulted in her lifetime, guess who's doing the assaulting?[3] Bingo. You guessed it—men, almost every single time.

When girls walk down the street and get cat-called, it's not by women. It's a man.

When girls are approached by people online who want nudes or send them unsolicited nudes, well, I hate to state the obvious, but its men doing the asking.

I'm not making this stuff up. These are facts. Almost every single time a female is approached, harassed, or cat-called, it's done by a male. And moms, chances are that you realize my words are true because it's likely happened to you a time or two. And I'm confident that the people who raised the men who cat-call women thought they were doing a fine job of raising good men, men who respected women, and yet they didn't. I get it. Nobody actively raises a harasser or abuser of women, or worse. There's not one parent out there who's hopeful and rooting for their son to grow up to be sexually perverted or violent.

Abuse toward women happens when young males are not raised in an environment that teaches them unequivocally that women are not merely sexual objects here on earth for their pleasure. Oh, I know, I know, you're probably going to come at me saying, "Well, then females on social media need to put some clothes on!" Or you might be the sort of person who thinks, "Well, men can't help their urges and if women are going to be so outwardly sexual, then they get what they get." To which I say, not so fast. And you're exactly who I need to have reading this chapter. Having sex with, and to that end, getting consent from a girl when you're a boy isn't that cut and dry. It's not about whether a girl gives your son "the vibe" that she wants sex, or because they're drinking at a party and are pressed up against one another when dancing.

These are not the "go ahead" signs for a boy to make a sexual move on someone. Sexual consent isn't up for interpretation. Sexual consent must be given, at all times, for sex to take place. It absolutely needs to be vocalized, and it is your job to teach this fact to your sons. It's not my place, or my daughters' place, or the daughters of the other parents who are reading these words to teach your sons about understanding consent. This responsibility falls entirely and squarely on your shoulders.

> Consent is your primary focus as a parent when teaching your kid about sex.

Do the work. And if you're the sort of parent who is desperately seeking out exactly how and what to teach your male child about understanding without a shadow of a doubt the signs of consent, I'm happy to direct you to a powerful book written by Cheryl Bradshaw, a fellow author friend of mine, titled *Real Talk About Sex and Consent*.

Run, don't walk, to get this book. It is a quick yet informative read about teaching your kids what true consent looks like. And listen, I'm not a dummy. I do realize that there are some females who have predatory tendencies. So, I encourage all parents to read this book to help you educate your children about how to recognize the signs of consent as well as how to be firm and communicate clearly when sex is something they don't want, even if it was something that they started out wanting.

You see, it can be tricky when young people have sex, well, too young. Once that train leaves the station, and all those hormones and urges are coursing through their veins, it becomes very difficult to stop. It feels so good, and they want to get to the other side of it, and how awesome would it be to actually FINALLY have an orgasm with a living, breathing person instead of their sock or washcloth or stuffed frog! It would be, and it is, but that other person must still be in the game with you. So, parents, it is your job to teach your kid to understand that *"no" is a complete answer* and that they cannot push somebody after they've said no, even if they said yes initially. Teach your teen that it is allowed, it's okay, and, more importantly, it's to be expected that a young sexual partner is likely to change their mind, and if/when they do, they must stop.

Consent is your primary focus as a parent when teaching your kid about sex. You must educate them on the other person's right to choose to pump the brakes at any point in time during a sexual encounter. It's not your child's right to coerce or manipulate their partner into going further than they are ready to go.

Do we have an agreement?

As a woman who's encountered too many males who were not raised this way, please take it from me—the mental damage done to the other person as a result of ignorance and entitlement is, for many, something from which can be impossible to return. I'm one of the lucky ones; I turned my abuse into my driving force. For many others, they don't get out of it as fortunate. So, please make a vow right now to have honest, soulful talks with your kids about sexual consent, and go get Cheryl's book!

## BEING SEXY AND SEXUAL DOESN'T MAKE YOU A SLUT

Now, this section is primarily for you parents of daughters, or people who identify as female. This next topic is a slippery slope, and as a mom to three girls, I have to say that I've honestly put my foot in it so many times that I truly thought I fucked it up beyond repair. The topic? How do you teach girls to own their sexuality without the outside world perceiving them as a "slut?"

Now, parents, you've probably been in a situation where you either were shamed by kids you went to school with, especially if you were raised in a liberal home and had zero hang-ups about sex (which then made most people around you afraid of you because that's not exactly "normal" in our still incredibly uptight society), or you may have been a person who judged and called your classmate names. Why? Because they were confident with their sexuality, they wore it, and they owned it. To be clear here, when I say liberal and confident, I'm talking about how a person identifies as well. It is brave and courageous to come out as a gender different than what you were assigned at birth. It is bold and scary and difficult to admit to the outside world that you are sexually attracted to and love someone of the same gender as yourself. It's complex and complicated to tell the world that you were born with male parts but know you're a woman, and vice versa. Kids who are wrestling with these truths know that a lot of the world isn't ready for them and that a significant part of the population won't accept them, and yet they're brave enough to step into their truths anyway.

Our job as parents is and always will be this: Raise your kids to be tolerant and accepting of others no matter who they are, how they identify, or what lifestyle they choose. Whatever that looks like, do it. But the easiest way is to . . .

Teach them to mind their business.

If they know a girl who likes to have sex, and is careful and smart with other consenting partners, that's her business, not your teen's or yours. Don't raise a "slut shamer." Don't get it twisted—our primary job as parents is to give our kids the deep-rooted understanding that what other people do in their lives is truly none of their business. That doesn't mean they need to understand the way somebody else chooses to live or be in agreement with how somebody behaves. Hell, they don't even have to hang out with them if they don't want to. Remember the single most important part of our job as parents is to raise our kiddos to be kind, accepting, and tolerant people. Our kids must recognize that they're not on this earth to judge, condemn, belittle, or change anybody else around them. Their only job in this life is to look after who *they* are in the world. They should be humble, have grace, and let people be who they are because the truth is, how others act and identify has no impact on who your teen is in the world. My husband and I raised three people to be all these things, and I know you can too!

## ABOLISHING THE SEXUAL DOUBLE STANDARD

As adults, parents, and educators, it is important for us to understand that the sexual double standard exists and to do away with perpetuating it. The sooner we do so the better, and healthier sex will be shared for all the generations to come. As a woman and a mother of three women, I have caught myself, more times than I care to admit, thinking judgmental thoughts against women who are sexually confident. I have been known a time or two to either say out loud or think to myself, "That woman is giving me serious slut vibes."

Why would I do that? I was not in her bedroom, and I was not a friend of hers, so where did I get off deciding that she looked like she had a lot of lovers? And even if she did, what's wrong with that? Honestly, take a moment and ask yourself that question. If a woman happens to have a lot of lovers, what's the big deal? I mean, as long as none of them are married to somebody else, that is. Infidelity is something I have zero tolerance for . . . but that's for the other book, the relationship one! We live in a patriarchal society where if men have many lovers, they are lauded, upheld, even thought of by women as a great Casanova in bed! Hell, there's even a TV show about it. Ever watch *The Bachelor*? Yes, there is also *The Bachelorette*, but don't we all recall how Hannah Ann got called a slut by one of her former contestants for admitting she had sex in the windmill? Meanwhile, in *The Bachelor* that followed right after her season, Peter took every girl he could into the fantasy suite.

Oh yeah, the good ol' fashioned sexual double standard.

Men are admired, revered, and dare I say desired for their sexual conquests, and women are shamed, tarnished, and labeled "whores" if they have more than a handful.

What? The? Fuck?

How does a man having many lovers make him desirable, but a woman having many lovers make her tarnished? Used? Dirty? The reality is, it doesn't. This double standard is a social construct created by the patriarchy that all of us, for some reason, still continue to uphold. A female who is sexually liberated isn't less worthy or valuable than a man who does the same. So, if you are the parents of a son, make sure that you teach him that women have the same rights to sexual pleasure, freedom, and enjoyment as they do. I'm sure you've all had at least one run-in with a father who has said, "Oh, Jonathan has had sex with fifteen girls since he got to university! That's a chip off the old block right there! Making his father proud!" or some version of this vaunting. I had one father say in front of me once, "My son is in his first year of university, and he's already had his first threesome. I'm in my forties and I still haven't had one." I couldn't believe my ears as he continued to brag to me, a mother of girls, about it.

How weird, right? And made all the weirder because he was jealous of his son accomplishing something sexual BEFORE he'd had the chance to do it. And then the cherry on top of this weird cake was that he is the father of a daughter. I wondered if we'd be having that same conversation if his daughter had come home one weekend and said, "Dad. Oh my god! You're sooooo not going to believe this! I just had sex with two boys at the same time! How cool is that?" or "Dad, I was at this party, and we all took turns giving blow jobs with different colored lipstick to a boy, and we made his penis look like a rainbow! It was soooo cool! Sort of like an art installation but on his dick!"

I can guarantee with my last dollar on the line that that father would not have had the same attitude about it AT ALL. But why not? The two girls in bed with his son, well, they are somebody's daughters, so men want *somebody's* daughters to be sexually liberated enough to engage freely in "out of the norm" sexual relations with *them*, just not the women connected to them. Not their daughters or sisters. And for some men, they don't even want their own wives to fully enjoy sex.

Parents, you need to know that this stuff happens, that females as young as twelve and thirteen are having parties like that. So, talk about sex. Ask your kids how much they know about sex, and if they've ever had a sexual experience. They might say they never have, and that's actually the truth, or they may have already done some stuff and think they'd be in trouble if you knew, but at least start the dialogue. Talk about sex early so you'll be the first to know when they're getting active, so you can ensure they're safe and making conscientious choices. The bottom line here is that it is as okay for our daughters to be sexually confident as it is for our sons.

## SEX AND STDS DON'T HAVE TO GO HAND IN HAND

No matter what your stance is on sex, even if you're preaching abstinence in your house, and that sex is only meant for procreation and not to be enjoyed, or that your daughter best be a virgin when she walks down that aisle, you need to wake up and be realistic.

Lord, oh Lord. So many parents have NO IDEA. The number of times my girls have told me about girls they know who are vaginal virgins but still do anal . . .

Yup. Cue confused emoji here.

Let that sink it.

I'm not here judging—to each their own in sex. I fully subscribe to and live this way of being. Wholeheartedly. If you have consenting people in a sexual relationship, it is not anybody's business but theirs what brings them both pleasure. Period. End of story.

But a group of young women not having vaginal intercourse but having anal instead? I'm shaking my head here. Parents, come on, do you see what your nonsense is creating? Sex is natural, it's normal, it's awesome. In fact, there are so many times when I've been depressed, or brokenhearted, or just having a brutal time finding joy in my life, then I'd have sex with my man, and I was like a new woman! It is one of the most amazing parts of being a healthy human being. But regardless of how many parents believe that their kids are really going to fully abstain, some will and some won't. In my years of being a mom, I've met many kids of both genders who are waiting—and that's a beautiful thing, and I applaud them. It's tough to do and incredibly commendable. Sex does complicate life/relationships and can be a major distraction, so ideally, yes, we want our kids to wait, to hold off until they're in a solid, healthy, mature relationship. We want their minds to be fully formed and their confidence to be embedded in other parts of their awesomeness.

That said, we need to educate our kids before they start having sex so they don't end up with a teen pregnancy or an STD. We must have conversations about safe sex. Be sure that your daughter always has her own condoms so that a guy can never say to her, "Oh, I don't have any, and it will be just this one time." And then there's the classic, "I'm clean. You're the only person I'm dealing with right now." The list of persuasive excuses goes on and on and on, so educate your kids about all of them. Teach your sons to have condoms readily available for their own safety as well as the safety of the sexual partners in their lives. Buy them condoms. Take them with you and have them buy them. I don't really care how you do it, but do it. Remember, the pill stops most pregnancies, but condoms reduce the spread of STDs including gonorrhea and chlamydia, and they lower the risk of contracting syphilis, herpes, and HPV.

> We must have conversations about safe sex.

So, let's just agree that we're teaching our kids to wrap it up and have safe and consensual sex. And if you're the parent of a girl and feel more concerned about a teen pregnancy, then get them on the pill pronto to help reduce that risk too.

At the end of the day, we can wish and hope that our kids aren't sexually active, but we must prepare them with information about consent and protection for when the time eventually comes!

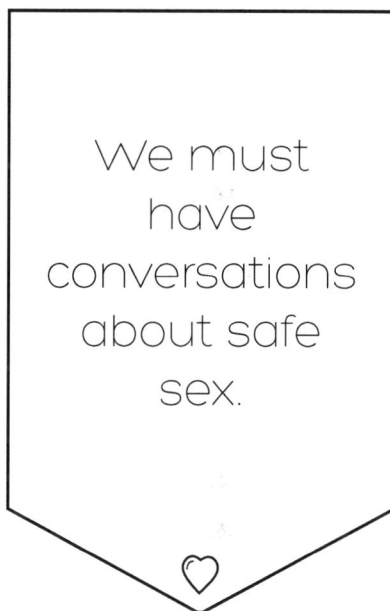

## WHEN YOUR TEEN IS STRUGGLING WITH SEXUAL PREFERENCE

Look, I'm not going to sit here and write a ton about helping your teen "come out." I can't write about it because I haven't lived it, and I would never, ever disrespect families, or teens, living this experience. My girls are female, and they identify as female. They're heterosexual women who enjoy sexual relations with heterosexual males. So, for me to sit here and give you direct advice on how to cope with this topic, how to navigate it, or how to support your child through it would be a tad arrogant on my behalf. Therefore, I am going to refrain from saying too much, except for what I have experienced through friends who have had kids come out, and that is this: The world is cruel enough. Though there's been progress made over the decades, it's not enough—there is still much fear, hatred, and prejudice against the LGBTQ+ community. The last thing your child needs from you, within their own four walls, is judgment or intolerance from their own parents who are supposed to love them and protect them. Regardless of what you think, I invite you to accept it with love. Even if you don't understand it, or don't agree with it, or it's against your values/beliefs, you get a lifetime to change your ideals and only one chance to be a safe place for your teen to land when the time comes for them to step into who they really are.

Think about that.

Leave the negative thoughts, worries, judgments, concerns, anger, fear—anything that is not rooted in love—for the conversations with your co-parent (behind closed doors), your friends, your own parents, your therapist. If you need to express all the dark, negative, and anxious thoughts and feelings you may be struggling with, do so outside of your relationship with your kid. The time may come when you can share with them how getting the news affected you, but for now, be their rock. Be a support. Be love. And if you're out of your depth, it's okay to seek help and support so that you, your kid, and your household can come to terms with the new normal in your family.

The common thread that most of my gay friends have shared with me about their own coming out was how incredibly scary it was for them. They had very real fears that their parents would no longer love them. In some cases, they were kicked out of their families, which is brutal. I cannot imagine not seeing one of my girls again because of the gender of who they love. Don't be that parent.

I beg, plead, and implore you to fight the good fight to be on side with your kid. Many of my gay friends have told me something along the lines of the following: "Coming out was a lose-lose situation. If I didn't, I would be living a lie my entire life. But if I did, I knew that life would be outwardly hard for me because a bulk of the world would never accept me, and in some cases, I would not be safe to walk around freely."

So, knowing that this is their reality, do you really want to create an unaccepting home environment too? Home is our safe haven, our refuge from the storm. You signed up to love your child unconditionally when you got pregnant, and you can't go back on that unspoken promise now. I mean you can—you can do whatever you want. But why would you want to?

# Things to Nibble On

♡ No matter your upbringing, it's now time to acknowledge that sex is a natural and normal part of being human. It's a parent's job to evolve from how they were raised; now's your chance to remove shame from sex. If you have deep-rooted issues with sex even now as an adult, get a sex therapist to help you release them so you don't dump that on your unsuspecting teen.

♡ When is the best time to talk to your kid about sex? Well, I happen to believe that organically having the sex talk as a regular part of your family life is the best way to address sex. If you're consistently dealing with the issue of sex in age-appropriate ways their entire lives, you'll never have to do that work-up-your-nerve, clear-your-throat, time-to-sit-down-and-get-to-it awkward conversation. Make sex a taboo subject, and your kids will learn about it from other sources; make it normal and natural, and they won't be running out the door to go and "get some." It's 2021, you all—it's time we teach our children that sex is a natural part of being human.

♡ I know I came at the parents of boys pretty hard here, but I said what I said–sexual assaults are almost always committed by the part of the population with penises. Therefore, the weight of teaching boys about consent, true consent, lands squarely on your shoulders. I know you can do it! I know you want your sons to be gentlemen. You don't want to wonder whether your son slid his hand up a girl's skirt at lunch. The only way to ensure that he doesn't is by educating him not to. So, if you haven't already done so, order Cheryl Bradshaw's book *Real Talk About Sex and Consent*–it is overflowing with insightful information. Now, parents of girls, don't think you shouldn't read this book or teach your girls about consent, because that's not at all true. Cheryl also talks about teaching our daughters to send clear messages to their sexual partners. Consent is a two-way street with both partners needing to know the signs and how to clearly speak the language. Get it, read it, discuss it with your teen, then have them read it too!

♡ Teach your teen to let people live their lives the way they want to, including their sexual lives. It is none of your kid's business who somebody loves, who somebody enjoys making out with, or how many intimate partners someone has had. The only person who those details should matter to is the person who is living that experience. Please do the world a favor and be committed to raising your teen to only worry about their own choices, decisions, and ideals. Let's be sure to not teach our kids to slut-shame or attack people who are sexually different.

♡ Rid your house of the double standard when teaching your kid about sex. Be sure that you're not perpetuating the whole narrative that men can be as sexual as they like but women cannot. I've witnessed dads share information about their sons having a nice-sized penis, but then see parents shame their daughters in front of outsiders about tight tops or the size of their breasts. First, let's not sexualize breasts–they do so much more than bring men sexual pleasure, but let's also not make a young woman feel any more insecure than she might already be feeling about large breasts. Let's just agree to be cool about the size of our kids' bits and pieces, shall we?

♡ Sex is awesome, pleasurable, and way more fun without STDs. Talk like a broken record about protection, and not just about how NOT to get pregnant but how NOT to end up with an STD, because although many can be cured with medication, many last with you for your entire life. So, teach your son to wrap it up for his own safety as well as his partner's.

♡ If you have a preteen/teen who you know is struggling with their sexuality, I appreciate that it must be so painful for you. As adults, we know how cruel the world can be, and if we didn't struggle with that ourselves, we may feel like we won't guide them through it well. My advice to you is to pull in an expert right away. It will save years of struggle for your kid and for you. No parent likes to see their child suffer. Get them the help they need to be supported in this journey.

♡ While we're on the topic of sex, now's a really great time for you to run a bath, unwind, then, you know . . . have some sex of your own!

.

*Chapter Six*

# DRUGS, VAPING, AND ALCOHOL

I have to tell you, I really hummed and hawed over writing this chapter, so much so that it was the last chapter I wrote; I left it until the very end. I wondered what I could share that you probably didn't already know. You either know firsthand the powerful addictive properties of smoking/vaping/alcohol/drugs or have an idea of it, at least. Maybe, like me, you grew up with it. Or maybe you got involved with it yourself at a young age and had a hard time breaking free. Whatever your story or convictions, I get it—all of this is so damn polarizing. I've not met a single parent in my thirty-two years of being one where someone has said to me, "I don't really have an opinion on whether I want Becky to do drugs, smoke, or drink. It doesn't matter to me what she does."

That has never happened. Parents KNOW how they feel about alcohol, drugs, and vaping. Chances are you fall into one of these two camps or maybe somewhere in the middle: "I don't care if they do or don't, it's their body" OR "I'll kill my kid if they ever need to be carried out of somebody's home because they've blacked out."

I'm hoping to do with this chapter what I've done throughout this book so far—help you parent with balance. For a lot of parents, this chapter will be super difficult to digest. In a world where marijuana is legal in places and alcohol consumption and binge drinking are on the rise, probably the most challenging lesson to teach our kids (because it is rooted in hypocrisy) is not to indulge. In my personal experience, there is no other part of my parenting journey that I feel was more "do as I say and not as I do" than when it came to the drugs/vaping/ smoking/alcohol years. It's a slippery slope. I will give you some tools to explain to your teens why these things are "okay" for you but not for them, which is mostly based in science and the damage that partaking in these activities has on the development of their brain, and I'll guide you in helping them understand why you're able to partake in legal, mind-altering, extracurricular party favors but they're not.

It's not easy to get kids through this stage of their teen years, but it can be done, and I know because my husband and I did it. The number of times we had to pick up our blacked-out girls from a basement party? Exactly zero. So, let's dig in.

## SMOKING, VAPING, AND THE CONSEQUENCES OF "BEING COOL"

Picture a group of pre-tweens in a ravine, tucked in a cluster of tall pine trees, laughing, chatting, and smoking.

Yup. Smoking. At age nine. That was me.

Smoking was glamorous. My mom did it; she could make smoke rings. I thought it was *so cool*. Characters smoked on all the TV shows. Adults smoked at restaurants, at stoplights in their cars, and while tanning on a chaise with sunglasses on. Man, oh man, did I ever want to be glamorous, cool, and all grown up. I also hung out with the older girls who lived in our apartment complex, and they smoked too. So, naturally, I had all the reasons to want to smoke, but I had no money because I was, well, nine. What was my work-around for this teeny, tiny detail? Because I was NOT mooching cigarettes from the older girls. Oh, hell no! I cleaned out my mom's ashtray, and instead of flushing the butts down the toilet (yeah, that was another thing we did back then so the trash wouldn't smell), I put them in a paper towel and hid them in my room for safekeeping until it was time to go hang in the ravine. I felt so smart and so cool, and I kept up this practice until I turned twelve and started working at the pizza joint in the mall making $2.10 an hour and was able to buy my own smokes.

I smoked on and off until I was fourteen, which was when my mother found out and said, "You can smoke, or you can dance. But I'm not paying for you to do something healthy for yourself while you do something to make you sick." I remember thinking, *If it's bad for me, and it's unhealthy, why do you do it?* But I didn't question my mom because I knew it was, in fact, bad for me. So, I stopped. I told my friends I had to quit so I could keep dancing. They were all dancers so they got it, and they each said they would have done the same thing if their mom had said what mine did. So, I got to be cool without giving myself the black lung before turning sweet sixteen.

Now, chances are your tweens/teens totally know how bad smoking and vaping are for them. I mean, back when I was little, we didn't know all the ramifications. Heck, it was still considered sexy, chic, and sophisticated to smoke. But kids nowadays know better. They see the ads—the ones targeted toward them to get them addicted as well as the ones that tell them doing this shit will likely make them very ill. Yet they do it anyway. So, what's a parent to do in this situation?

Well, I don't know what you're going to do, or what you feel is the right thing to do, but I told my girls over and over again not to smoke or vape. Did they listen? Well, yeah, for a good long while. And then high school came, and so did weed and occasional smoking. But what really stuck for them was when they got with some friends, and their vape oil tasted like watermelon, and before I knew it, they were vaping. I was overruled. Now, I could have lost my mind, and I could have grounded them, but they were already out of high school and in university, so that would have been pretty difficult. So, I did the only thing I could do at that point in time in my parenting journey. I prayed that all the good senses I'd instilled in them would make them come to those good senses and they'd stop on their own.

And you know what? That's precisely what they did. They quit on their own. And I didn't have to beat them or harp on them.

Some battles in parenting require you to retreat and let your kids exhaust themselves by going it alone and doing what they think is right. These are the toughest days, or at least they were for me, but they were worth it. Your kids get to a certain age when you have to stop raising them, stop coaching them, and stop telling them how to be and just trust that you've put enough strength of character into them that they will come out of an unhealthy situation intact. Now, obviously, if they're hooked on meth or fentanyl,

> There are situations you need to let them learn on their own.

you're not going to step aside, but you know what I'm saying and what I mean. There are situations where you need to let them learn on their own after you've given them your advice. You may have a different way you'd like to tackle these situations, and to that I say, good luck and stick to your guns, whatever those may be!

## THE GLAMOROUS LIFE OF PUKING IN YOUR BOOTS AT A PARTY

You've probably done it a time or two yourself. Maybe not in your boots, but for sure in a toilet, in a bush, or on your lap when you had that last drink that put you right over the edge of being able to "hold your booze." We've all been there. I mean, this is a massive assumption that I'm making, but we have, haven't we? If you haven't, I'd love to know how you managed it.

I grew up with a dad who often drank to the point of puking. And the worst part of it was that he would puke and then drive himself home. Those were wild, wild days, back before there were strict drinking and driving laws. I'm just thankful that he never killed anybody. He was in accidents, but nobody (other than my older brother) ever got hurt. And that was by the grace of God I say, because the man drove drunk *a lot*.

Because of my upbringing, alcohol didn't appeal to me. It certainly wasn't glamorous to me the way smoking had been. I saw the ugly, dirty, violent side of booze, which kept me as far away from it as possible. I didn't have my first drink until I was eighteen, then didn't really drink again until my late twenties and early thirties. Once my girls hit double digits, I began to drink. I was hanging out with other parents, and martinis were a new thing to me. Alcohol stealthily and silently slipped into my life. When I realized I had begun drinking daily, I encouraged myself to stop, or at least slow my roll. I still didn't think it was a problem until I noticed that my adult daughters were drinking daily too.

*What?!*

And that's when I realized that my casual "they drink wine with every meal in Europe" attitude was not the road I wanted to travel down anymore.

That was November 2020. So, do the math: I had almost eighteen years of being sophisticatedly buzzed. When I added up how much drinking was costing me, and looked in the mirror at what it was costing my body, and looked at my girls, I had an aha moment: I may have never picked them up off a basement floor at somebody's home, but I had imparted that it was perfectly fine to consume this poison daily. And I was embarrassed. I felt immense guilt that I had raised them that way, so what did I do?

Well, I practiced what I preached and told them that I had made a mistake—I was wrong for raising them to think of alcohol as their reward for passing that test, for getting the job, for getting through a tough day. I was wrong for making it a symbol of celebration and pleasure. I vowed to be different. I stopped drinking alcohol because stopping was good for me, for them. I said I was wrong and that I was sorry, then I changed. Alcohol is no longer a part of our daily lives, and you know what? We get along better. We don't have emotional explosions in the middle of seemingly innocent conversations. We sleep better. We communicate more deeply, and contrary to what I thought would happen, we did not all become boring. We laugh more! We have the energy to do more. It's amazing. I never would have thought casual drinking was robbing so much from our family until, well, until we all stopped drinking every damn day.

Although I'm not someone who has ever considered herself an alcoholic, and I thought my liberal approach to drinking was good for my girls, if I could do it all again, I would still allow my daughters to drink as teens for three reasons:

1. They never got hammered to the point of blacking out.
2. They knew their limits.
3. They didn't sneak around getting drunk at all hours of the day because they thought drinking alcohol was a taboo or mysterious thing to do.

Now, what you want to do with your tweens/teens is totally up to you. I respect that they're your kids, that you have your house rules, and all that. If you happen to be leaning heavily to the side of "over my dead body" and "they will live to rue the day . . . " about alcohol in your household, I encourage you to think back to when you were a teen and remember all the things your parents said no to. Chances are that you only wanted those things more. So, moderation may be the better play here, my friends, rather than fire and brimstone.

It's all about balance—living in the middle ground of parenting your teen.

If you are one of those parents who is trying to grow your own living, breathing, live-in drinking buddy with your teen, I encourage you to read the book *Drink* by Ann Dowsett Johnston. It is powerful, educational, and so convicting that I had to put the book aside while in the height of my denial about my alcohol consumption. It was profoundly eye opening and deeply convicting. If you're on the fence about your need to stop drinking daily and need a push in a healthier direction, then this is the book to get the job done.

## THE SEDUCTION OF DRUGS

Drugs. Drugs. Drugs. They're everywhere. Your kids' favorite music artists do them, vapes are sold at the corner store, and you may even smoke some weed now that it's pretty much legal everywhere. You can't escape them. Drug use is completely normalized, and yet our kids are not supposed to do them.

"Drugs are bad for you."

"There are going to be severe consequences if I ever catch you doing them!"

We say these things to our kids with a martini or a cigarette in our hand. Hell, we may have even had both in our hand while we gave them the "Do as I say and not as I do speech" for the millionth time. I know you've given your kids this speech because I'd given it to my girls too. I was famous for lecturing about the dangers of drugs, yet meanwhile, I was smoking hash four times a week and drinking apple martinis nightly.

Oh yeah, I was a shining example of motherhood.

I said it in my first book, and I'm saying it ad nauseum in this book: If I could fuck up all the ways that I did with raising my girls and still manage to make decent human beings, then you, who I am totally confident is NOT smoking hash multiple times a week or drinking on the daily, should hit this parenting ball right out of the park!

And even though I'm confessing to you right now, I'm likely going to receive a ton of letters in the mail about my stance on drugs. I know so many parents who say, "A little weed here and there is no big deal. It's not going to do them any harm" or "Marijuana is not a gateway drug to anything; that's some BS that I don't buy into. I smoked weed as a teen, and I still smoke it now, and I'm not on the corner smoking crack because of it. I have no problem with my kid smoking pot." Then there's the parent who actually smokes it in front of their children, and there are even some (and you may find this difficult to believe if your kids haven't entered tweendom) who smoke *with* their kids.

Now, I can totally say that I smoked weed with my two oldest girls when they were both in university. It happened once, and to be honest, it was a lot of fun. So, I can't sit here all righteous and say that you should have your children taken from you, unless, of course, they are a minor. In that case, I strongly feel smoking marijuana with your minor is poor parenting and irresponsible, and I do not recommend doing so for many reasons. But once they're their own people, of legal smoking and drinking age, if you want to smoke with them on occasion, that's your choice. I mean, you may sit and drink with them, and both alcohol and marijuana are mind-altering products, so it's basically a "pick your poison" roulette game.

And it is poison. Even though marijuana comes from a plant, and so many of you are "for it," there is so much scientific evidence as to why, as a parent, you need to reconsider your leniency toward weed. I mean, this topic in and of itself could make up an entire book, but since I don't have that sort of knowledge, I'm going to direct you to some further reading. I'm an advocate for critical thinking and digging into things that we might be on the fence about to glean our own knowledge. I mean, we're not

As a parent, you need to reconsider your leniency toward weed.

sheeple here, are we? Read up, friends, don't just take my word for why weed is not a great thing for your kid to casually smoke while their brains are developing. Apparently, the weed my mother says she didn't smoke during the Woodstock era had like 1–3 percent THC (the compound responsible for its psychoactive effects) in it, and now, the record for most THC in Canada (during the writing of this book) is 30 percent by an Alberta company that goes by the name Kade's Kush under the brand High Tide (according to Leafly.com).

Parents, that is a massive jump. This shit will fuck you up. So, to be clear here, folks, kids aren't just getting stoned anymore—they're getting totally fucked up. And these massive levels of THC aren't only getting them extremely high, they're also causing psychotic episodes. Recent data collected by the European Monitoring Center for Drugs and Drug Association found that people who smoke pot daily are *three times more likely* to experience a psychotic episode than someone who hasn't used the drug. Additionally, kids younger than fifteen who start smoking pot have an even more elevated risk of experiencing psychosis.[4]

With any controversial topic, you will have believers and nonbelievers. There were some studies I came across that mentioned that the data isn't there to simply blame high levels of THC on why some kids develop psychosis with regular THC exposure. And while I can see that to be the case, there will always be the argument that genetics or preexisting conditions may or may not have played their role in presenting the extremely adverse side effect of a mental breakdown or the development of schizophrenia. I mean you say tomato, I say toe-ma-toe. But here's the bottom line: I happen to have witnessed ten different boys who were chronic, daily weed smokers from the time they were fourteen until their early twenties, and every single one of them had some sort of mental breakdown. The breakdown was so bad for one of them that he was institutionalized. A couple of the other boys, who were honor roll students, dropped out of university. And a few others couldn't function enough to even get to university. I don't know your genetics, I don't know the stability of your child's brain or their chemical makeup, so I can't sit here and tell you that your kid will totally have an adverse side effect to THC. But I can't say that they won't, either. I am not a brain expert. What I can write in this book is my suggestion/ recommendation for what to do with your kids: Raise them in a home environment that is completely open, honest, transparent, and loving. Share the statistics. Explain how drug use affects young brains. Express your concerns, and always, always guide them to the "proof is in the pudding" side of an argument.

You need to decide early on with your co-parent what your expectations are around drug use. And because we are best friends now, let's be honest with one another here: You and your co-parent may have, at one time or another, engaged in casual/recreational drug use. Perhaps you currently use. If you do, your teen likely knows, which means you'll have your work cut out for you when you try and explain to them why it's okay for you to partake, but they can't. For example, "I can smoke this insanely potent weed because my brain has finished forming, so I'm not at risk in the same way you are" or "I am a responsible adult with a career, a roof over my head, and a healthy relationship. I'm mature and know when enough is enough. Because you're younger than I am, and you're 'not there yet,' it's in the best interest of your personal development to not smoke weed when you're so young."

Kids are uber clever these days, and they're not going to simply not do something because you asked them not to, so you need to break down to them why it's okay for you to do certain things but not them. Remember what I've been saying throughout this entire book: clear, honest, genuine communication is how you'll end up being able to guide your teen to listen to your rules, and not just listen to them, but *follow* them. And then, after you've told them that drugs are not allowed, you will need to be extra clear and confident as to what the consequence will be should you have a child who ends up using. Who will you pull in to help ensure that your child's casual drug use doesn't turn into a full-on addiction while you allow them to "experiment" with weed for too long? You need to have your plan in place now before you're faced with this possible challenge in your parenting journey. After all, it doesn't do you any good to put on your oxygen mask after the plane has crashed, now does it?

Be prepared. Be organized. Be involved with your kid. Start talking about drugs NOW. What do they know about drugs? Do they have any questions about drugs? Do they know anybody who uses drugs? Hang out with your kid, engage them in open conversations about what is going on in the world around them, in music, on TV, and in real life at school. Be their safe space to land. Be their person.

And if you find yourself in the thick of a drug issue that is taking over your kid right now, I'm so sorry that you're going through this difficult and painful time. I'm pretty certain that while you were cuddling with them all those years ago that you never imagined that you would find yourself here with them. My heart goes out to you, and I truly wish you all the success in the world in getting your child off drugs. If you're lost and don't yet have a plan of attack on how you're going to save your beautiful child, may I make a few suggestions of what I would do if I were in your position?

1) Get professional help right away. Pull somebody in immediately who deals with addiction for a living. (If you haven't done this already.)

2) If you don't have the means to hire a private addiction counselor,

then contact your local help lines. A simple Google search will help you locate the contact information for your area.

I've witnessed some friends admit their children into rehab facilities, while others attempted to get their kids clean all on their own. Some have succeeded, while others have failed. I truly hope that you end up a success story. I'm rooting for you!

## Things to Nibble On

♡ It's 2021. Quit smoking so your kid won't smoke. I mean, the science is in. Smoking, vaping, and all the nicotine habits cause cancer. Period. Don't let your kid smoke.

♡ Don't make drinking alcohol "taboo." We all know that the more you tell a tween/teen not to do something, the more they will.

♡ Drugs have an insidious side to them. There, I said it. Honestly, I cannot stress enough how strongly I feel that the conversation with your kids about drugs should be started as early as possible. They need to know the dangers, the risks, and the consequences of drug abuse. Additionally, there needs to be a very real conversation with your co-parent about house rules on drugs and what happens if/when drugs enter your home.

♡ Where smoking/vaping/alcohol/drugs are concerned, you need to be ready for them. You need to have a battle plan in place so you're prepared to fight this war should you need to. You don't want to be blindsided. Build a course of action with your parenting partner that you implement the second you find out that your kid is using any of these substances. And listen, you didn't hear it from me, but if you have suspicions that your kid is using, there's nothing wrong with doing a little "walk through their room" or "search through their bag" for evidence. If they're not using, then you will obviously find nothing, and if they are, well, let's just say they're going to call you all sorts of names for finding them out. The way I always looked at it with my girls is that I didn't carry them in my womb and deliver them so they could do something foolish that could potentially end their lives. Whether you birthed your child or not, I know you can relate. Having them hate you for a while is nothing compared to the alternative.

♡ I'd tell you to have sex, but, honestly, I've been here in your shoes, and if you're dealing with any one of these things, you're not in the mood for sex! But tomorrow is another day, my friend, and even if you're not feeling it, trust me when I tell you, YOU ARE DOING GREAT!

*Chapter Seven*

# THE SHIT WILL HIT THE FAN

You've made it this far, friend! I get it; this book is pretty heavy, and if you're just over the hump of double digits, and this kid is your oldest, this stuff may be hitting you hard. You're probably feeling overwhelmed at the potentially negative, and in some cases, life-threatening situations you may find your kid living with during their teen years. I'm not here to freak you out; I'm not here to blow your world apart. I'm here to be truthful, to present you with the possible scenarios that may occur with your teen. And listen: You can choose to get through the teen years any way you want. I hate to admit it, but I've witnessed some parents literally do nothing at all when their teen drove drunk or skipped classes or lied about their whereabouts or hid their drug use. I've watched parents live the ostrich life, and so far, their kids are still alive and haven't killed anyone by driving high or drunk. They're all living quite happily. And that might be the route you decide to take after you read my stories about how I got my girls to their midtwenties and into their thirties intact and without ever having operated a motor vehicle while drunk. You might think, "You know what, Shantelle? Thanks for the wisdom and thanks for the stories, but I'm going to play it fast and loose with my kid." And off you'll go on your merry way, and I'll truly wish you the utmost success. I pray that your children have their own impeccable moral compasses, that they'll do no harm, and that no harm comes to them. I really and truly do. But should you happen to think that I just may be on to something, then I invite you to continue reading, because you may not have a kid who dabbles in drugs, smoking, vaping or alcohol, but you could end up with one who is a chronic liar, or with one who struggles with mental health issues, an eating disorder, or self-harms. So, this chapter may be one that you need somewhere down the road of your parenting journey.

So, let's talk about shit hitting the fan. Your baby, your cherub who once used to love morning cuddles, homemade meals, and chatting with you, has now, seemingly overnight, turned into a teen who won't even look you in the eye over the breakfast table. The only response you ever receive from them is a grunt, or a monosyllable (if you're lucky). If this is your new morning ritual, you're not alone, and it's not about you, it's about them. Your kid is changing, there are a bajillion hormones coursing through their veins, and it affects their behavior. And even though you may want to take it personally, I urge you to step back and see it through the lens of what used to be. Think about it: How did you act in the mornings as a teen?

Maybe you were a regular ray of sunshine like Reese Witherspoon in *Election*, or maybe you were a horse pill in the morning. However you acted, I want you to take a moment and remember what it's like being a teenager. There's no need to be all doom and gloom and "what did I do to deserve this?" Don't go there. Don't get all dramatic and make your kid's attitude about you. It is about them—give them some space to work it out. Your kid is not doing anything *to* you. You're likely the last thing on their mind, believe me. It might be all those hormones racing through their veins, or they probably have stress about school. Maybe it's peer pressure. A crush. Confusion about their sexuality. So, how about you be the bigger person? Be the cooler person by loving them better and giving them a safe space to figure out their shit. Don't add to their pressures by constantly asking, "Are you okay? Is it something I did? Why won't you talk to me?"

Nag.

Nag.

Nag.

I learned the hard way. I'm a big-mouth. I talk a lot, and I ask a lot of questions. But don't worry, I'm not a one-sided person. As much as I ask my girls all sorts of questions, I never do so without sharing my own good, juicy information. The problem is that I want to know more about my kids than they want to know about me. So, I've learned to ask fewer questions and to wait until

> It is your job to play both parent and detective.

they are ready to come to me and share information. Learn from me, my friends—don't dump your drama and insecurities on their already burdened shoulders. They're trying to survive teendom, people, so give them some fucking space!

To be clear, giving them space is not at all the same thing as letting them get away with their shit. Riding them about not wanting to chat over breakfast doesn't warrant them telling you to stuff your oatmeal

up your ass, and it should be addressed. But this behavior is NOT the shit hitting the fan. When I say the shit will hit the fan, I'm talking about things like:

## LYING

I don't care what your socioeconomic background is. I don't care what religion you practice, or what gender you are, or which race. None of these things matter when it comes to teaching your child the common, basic human character trait that every parent should instill in their child: You do not lie. You are always honest. You tell the truth. It's as simple as teaching them when they're little not to cut the line.

You taught them that, right? You taught them not to cut lines in the same way you taught them to share, to be kind, to not judge others, and to wait their turn. Right? In my humble mom opinion, teaching your child to speak the truth falls into the same category as all these other traits you want your lover, your partner, your co-worker, and your friend to have. You definitely don't want your kid to be that person who cuts ahead of other cars in traffic, leaving others muttering, "Fucking asshole, what makes you so special that you should cut everybody off who's been waiting at the same red light as you for their entire lives?"

Nothing makes that person better than any other person driving on the road with them. You know that. I know that. And deep down inside, they also know that.

But they cut you off anyway. That's called entitlement.

It is a good thing to have standards your children need to live up to in order to make them excellent global citizens. It makes them the sort of people that other people like and want to hang out with to the point that they will eventually marry them and take them off your hands.

So, if you expect these sorts of basic human behaviors from every other person who is in your life circle, why would you raise a person to go out in the world without any of them?

I'll leave you with that for a few minutes.

The short answer? You wouldn't.

If you have a teen and you haven't instilled any of these character traits in them, now is the time to get humble, and fast. Now is the time to sit them down and be brutally honest with them. Let them know that you're sorry, that you're not perfect, and that you want them to know that you realize that you did them dirty, but now you're changing your ways, which includes no more lying.

When I was thirteen, I told my mom that I was sleeping at a friend's house, and I ended up spending half the night on the roof of a school with her. Don't ask me why we did it. It still makes zero sense to me, but I was a chronic liar. And it's not because my mom didn't teach me not to lie, she did teach me. All the time. But, you know, some kids, even though you tell them one million times to be honest, they just don't have it in them. They love to spin a tale or two. All is not lost, however . . . they could become best-selling authors! Look at me.

My mom did everything she could to ensure I was a "good kid." Even still, I wasn't. At the time. Yet when the rubber hit the road, when it was time for me to be a grown-up, I became an amazing human being. All the things she taught me, instilled in me, impressed on me, were all in there. So, don't lose hope, parents. Don't get to the point of throwing in the towel with your kid. There may be some days/weeks/months/ YEARS where you look at them and think, "They're just bad. I don't have it in me any more to fight with them to do the right thing. I give up." Don't. Keep going. Be consistent. Stay on the front line. Do the work. Put in the time. Love them more. Trust me, it worked on me, and it worked on one of my girls as well. The work pays off. You just can't quit halfway through the job.

Keep going. You'll see the fruit of your labor. Of this, I am sure.

So, when I tell you that your kid is never too young to ask them honest questions about what they're getting up to, remember this passage of my book, and picture me, at nine smoking cigarette butts in the ravine, or at thirteen on the school roof. Kids are curious, and they will get up to some shit! It is your job to play both parent and detective. Lucky for me, I did pretty much everything bad that a kid could do, so I was totally comfortable asking each of my girls point-blank questions about what the hell they were doing, which is why I suggest that you just ask your kid the questions, and if they lie, you let them know that you have busted their cool by showing them the receipts. The receipts may be in their Instagram stories or on their Snapchat. The point is to let them know you're on to them. With teens, you must always be one step ahead of them. Keep them guessing how you know all that you know so they think twice about trying to be sly with trying to get away with some shit. The reality is that once you've discovered a pattern of lying with your teen, or inappropriate online behavior, you must now become the parent who doesn't allow them to be on their devices in their rooms with their doors closed. If they're under the age of consent, you really should have access to their online lives, and homework on their laptops should be done where you can see them and their screens . . . IMO. Some of you may be thinking that I'm some autocratic, batshit crazy, hypervigilant, over-the-top police officer and not a parent, so I encourage you to do a little bit of research about online predators. Ask your friends with older kids how many times their children have been bullied via social media, been sent unsolicited dick pics, or how many creepy old men are propositioning them on the internet.

It's wild out there. It's not so much about them being dishonest about what they're up to out in the world but what the world is up to around them. And as a sexual abuse survivor, hell yeah I'm hypervigilant. My experiences have led me to be way, way, WAY more cautious than your average momma bear, but when the stats reveal that one in three girls will survive a sexual assault and one in five boys will, I'd say it's worth you becoming a little less laissez-faire by making sure your kids are telling you the truth about who their friends are.[5] Where they're going. Who they're hanging out with, both in the real world and the virtual one. Nobody ever had their lives completely altered by somebody caring too much, or loving them too thoroughly, or asking them the tough questions. But by being too casual, too easy, too "let them figure it out" or "I trust them, I don't want to micromanage them . . . ," if that's your parenting technique, I urge you to rein it in just a little.

One way we kept an eye on our girls online social activities was when they were younger and wanted to use the computer, we had their computer screen facing toward me so I could see it from where I was cooking dinner. And even though I monitored them, they still got up to some nonsense, which I will not get into here because this is not their life story, this is a parenting tome. I will respect their rights to their privacy. But trust me when I say that you will still run into problems, even when you're diligent and raising them with the expectations of mutual respect, trust, openness, and fairness. Think back to your teen years. You weren't always truthful. Whether it was a little white lie or a big ol' chunky one, chances are there was a time or two (or a million) that you bent your story to suit the desired outcome. So, parents, remember who you were, then exercise both patience and grace. Should you catch your teen in a flat-out lie, don't flip out. Don't go at them guns all blazing. Take a moment to collect yourself, remind yourself of your younger you, then talk to them like the adult you want them to become. Ask them why they felt the need to lie in the first place. Ask them why they thought they couldn't speak truthfully about what they wanted or where they wanted to go or who they wanted to see.

Parenting doesn't need to be a huge drama or drain. It really can be calm, cool, and straightforward. It's all in how you want to build it. You are in total and utter control of the relationships you build with every single one of your kids. You are the captain of your ship. Your children are passengers, so don't let the dynamic shift to where you feel like your ship is being steered by a hormonal teen lacking in life experiences.

That kid is not the captain.

Read that out loud.

Can you imagine a giant-ass cruise ship with a captain who is twelve, or maybe sixteen? You'd be like "Oh, hell no. I'll keep my feet on shore, thanks."

Right? I mean none of us would get on that boat. So, don't let that kid run your household, either.

The reality of being a parent of a fellow human who is trying to find their identity and determine who they are going to be in the world is that there will be more times than you're comfortable with that they will lie to you. It's a fact. Even if you know that you for sure did absolutely everything 100,000 percent right with them when they were little. So why are they lying to you now? Why? Why? Why?

Because, like I've been telling you, it isn't about you. It is about THEM. Step aside. Step back and realize that their journey is theirs alone. No matter what you did or didn't do, chances are they are still going to lie from time to time. They have to flex their independent muscles, check out their perimeters, and push those boundaries to see what it is they can get away with in the world. Listen, this is the thing about the family home—it is where they practice their act. Remember at large family get-togethers when the cousins used to create plays that they wanted all the parents to watch? Come on, I know you remember. I know you did this. I honestly don't think there is a single child on the planet who hasn't forced a grown-up, or two, or twenty to watch the dance they created with a cousin or sibling.

This is the same practice they participate in when it comes to lying. They say one little lie to check and see what the fallout will be. Is anybody going to catch it? And if they do, what's the consequence?

Our kids practice every single element of developing into a grown-up on us first. The bottom line is that the little white lies we let slip today (because they're sort of cute) have a greater impact on the type of human being our kid becomes. Whether their intent is sinister or innocent, it is our job to be on our A game and catch them and guide them to be their best selves. After all, your kid will eventually become somebody's partner. Don't you want them to be an awesome one? And let's take this parenting game one step further. Not only will your kid become somebody's lover, partner, and other half, but they will (should they choose to) become somebody's parent. And it is this reason, my friends, why you MUST be the best parent you can be in order for them to grow into the best parent they can be. Therefore, parents, put the work in now while it matters and before it's too late.

Now, another bridge you might have to cross as a parent is mental health issues.

## DEPRESSION AND OTHER MENTAL HEALTH ISSUES

It is important to know as the parent of a tween/teen that you will deal with mood swings, and some dark moods may last for days on end; I mean, I think we all know to expect this along the way. In my experience, as the mother of my girls, I have to say it was, in fact, quite normal for them to fall silent, to want more alone time, to close their doors and spend time listening to music, to talk endlessly to friends on the phone, or to not talk to anybody. The grumpy, cranky, bitchy days could seemingly go on and on and on *and on*. I also have to be completely open and honest with you—it was zero fun. It was the fucking worst. Yannick and I never knew how long the dark moods would last, or who would take the brunt of them. The feeling of walking on eggshells became common in our household during the teen years. Mostly it was poor Yannick who couldn't tell which end was up. It's no wonder he took up a sport that allowed him to spend hours upon hours alone in the woods.

If you think a problem is becoming chronic, and if you have a family history of mental illness/ depression, get help quickly.

I'm here to tell you that teens get depressed. It is, dare I say, quite normal. They can be depressed because a best friend has started to get closer to somebody else, and they are feeling left out. They might be blue because of their first breakup. Or maybe they're not doing well in school. Or perhaps you and your partner have ended your marriage/relationship. There are many reasons why a tween/teen can have a bout of depression. Did it rain on a day they wanted to wear new shoes? BAM, they might get depressed over that.

There is often no rhyme or reason, so do yourself and your kid a favor and don't get in their face about it. Don't ask them a bunch of questions: "What's wrong? Is there something I can do to help?" Ask a couple of questions, and ask only once, accept the responses they give you, then give them space.

However, keep in mind that you only give them space if their depression isn't chronic. If you notice that their depressive state starts lasting longer and longer and they aren't participating in their regular activities—ones they usually enjoy—get concerned. If they stop doing the things they used to love, prefer to eat alone, or are no longer hanging out with friends, these may be signs of a serious issue.

Here are some early behavior changes to watch out for in your teen that may indicate the onset of a mental illness:

- missing classes or extracurricular activities
- poorer performance on tests
- decreasing interest in personal hygiene
- becoming lethargic and withdrawn
- pronounced mood swings
- dropping existing friends and hanging around with others whose behavior is questionable[6]

I need to emphasize here that I don't know your kid, I don't know your genetics, and I don't know your family history, so I can't give you definitive answers about mental illness. Plus, I'm not qualified to. What I will tell you, because I lived it, is that if you think a problem is becoming chronic, and if you have a family history of mental illness/ depression, get help quickly. We did with our girls. I have dealt with depression and anxiety, and I didn't receive any support, which led to me dealing with, well, pretty much every single topic in this chapter. So, act swiftly like we did with our girls. We pulled in an expert very early on when the depression no longer happened around their periods but started to bleed into nonhormonal times of the month. We knew we didn't know how to diagnose or help them, so we enlisted the help of people who could. And then we left it up to our girls to decide when they felt like they had received enough support/tools to manage their mental well-being on their own.

In our home the conversation about mental health was an open, candid, and honest one. We did everything we could to create a safe space for our girls to share about their mental health struggles, and no matter how insignificant they felt the "trigger" was, we did our absolute best to help them to feel heard by really listening and not judging.

As a parent, I have not experienced firsthand the damage of severe mental illness with any of my girls. But as a friend, I have supported others through incredibly challenging mental health concerns with their kids, and I must say the one thing they all did right was seek immediate help when the issues presented themselves as more than just teen angst. I recommend you do the same. It's your best chance of getting your child to the other side of it, healthier and stronger. We must do everything in our power to ensure that our kids grow into mentally, emotionally, and physically healthy adults with the tools they need to go out into the wild on their own and not simply survive but thrive.

## DISORDERED EATING

Some parents of boys might see this topic and have the urge to skip it with the belief that eating disorders only affect girls, that they are a female issue perpetuated by fashion magazines, social media, and unspoken (and sometimes spoken) peer pressure from friends. Untrue. The National Eating Disorders Association cites that 20 million women and 10 million men will have an eating disorder in their lifetime.[7] And that's just in the United States. Wow, right? Additionally, males make up 25 percent of people with anorexia, and because they are typically diagnosed later than females, they are at higher risk of dying from this mental illness.[8] And it is a mental illness, folks. Eating disorders were added to the Diagnostic and Statistical Manual of Mental Disorders in 1980.

I developed bulimia when I was seventeen years old. I was ripe for the picking for an eating disorder. Boys started feeling me up when I was ten. I was raped at age twelve, and I was sexually assaulted by a family member shortly after that until I was fifteen. My dad was an abusive alcoholic who was in and out of our lives, and we lived paycheck to paycheck whenever he was gone. There was so much stress in my day-to-day life, and there were so many things completely and utterly out of my control.

There were two things I loved very much once I got into high school, the first of which was a brand-new dance studio where I took classes. The owner was so young, so pretty, so hip and cool. All our routines were choreographed to the most popular music on the radio, whereas my last studio had been all jazz and, well, old people's music because my instructor had been old. But at this new studio, we did musical theater, singing, and dancing. I finally felt like I was on Broadway! We reenacted *Cats* and Michael Jackson's *Thriller*—dry ice, tombstones, and all. It was awesome! I couldn't have been happier, until I wasn't. I started noticing that the only girls who got the dance solos were just like our teacher: tall and skinny. Like abnormally skinny. I started to take stock and deduced if I ever wanted to be in the front, I had to get thin, like really thin. Not the one hundred and fifteen pounds I was at five feet four. Clearly, that was not skinny enough; I had to get smaller than that. But how? I'd never dieted before. I don't recall even thinking about what I did or didn't eat, or how much food I should or shouldn't have. The only thought about food I had prior to that fateful time for me was simple: Did I like it or not? If I did, I ate it, and if I didn't, I didn't eat it. What I have come to learn now that I'm an adult is that the actual reason I didn't get put in the front is because I wasn't a very good dancer. At all. I had a hard time retaining the choreography, and I couldn't jump off the floor for the life of me. But, at the tender ages between fourteen and seventeen, I decided that not being in the front was due to my weight.

The second thing I loved was my high school boyfriend. He was a jock. A hockey and volleyball player. Imagine if Brad Pitt and Matt Damon made a child—that is what my high school boyfriend looked like, with Billy Idol hair. Tons of girls wanted to date him, including one of my best friends, but for some reason, he picked me. I felt like I'd won the lottery, until I didn't. He came from an even more dysfunctional homelife than I did (if that was possible) and had zero tools for being a good human. I mean, he did the best he could with what he had, I'll give him that, but honestly, he wasn't a very healthy first stab at love for somebody with as many issues as I had. One time when he broke up with me, he said it was because I had "thunder thighs" and then promptly turned around and dated a girl who, looking back now, probably had an eating disorder. She was also younger than I was. This was my perfect storm. Rejection thrust me into the world of bulimia, and before long, I was down to ninety-three pounds.

You know what happened when I got down to ninety-three pounds? I was cast as the lead for our dance school's musical portion of our year-end recital, and my boyfriend came back. So, I was rewarded. Validation and justification are just a couple of the problems with eating disorders (ED).

Now, you may be thinking to yourself, "My kid will never get an eating disorder because they have never been sexually or physically abused" or "My kid lives in a home with both their parents, and we have a healthy, happy homelife" or "My child is an athlete and athletes know they need to be strong so would never develop an ED." Friends, kids with EDs can come from any home, in any situation, so it's best to stay informed.

Knowing what signs to keep an eye out for will save you from potentially getting blindsided by the disease later, or sooner, since kids as young as eight years old are being seen for ED at the Hospital for Sick Children in Toronto. And as somebody who still battles hers every single day of her life, I can say that you don't ever fully recover from them, they don't ever leave you, and they're always there, whispering in the background and trying to lure you in again. It is a fight of a lifetime, and I encourage you to do some research because knowledge is power. We spend so much time reading and researching about all the other things we think are important in raising our kids: schools, tutors, sports/teams. All the things. I urge you, as somebody who lived it and had a mother who had no idea what the signs were until she caught me throwing up, to be informed. Knowledge can save your child's life.

So, if you're wondering if your child has an unhealthy relationship with food/their body, here are some classic symptoms to look out for. Keep in mind that each eating disorder will have their own unique symptoms, but there are some universal signs that straddle all of them.

**Physical Signs:**
- rapid weight loss or frequent dieting
- fainting or dizzy spells
- difficulty focusing/concentrating

- fatigue and insomnia
- low energy/lethargy
- irregular/absent menstrual cycle
- decreased libido for males
- swelling around the jaw or cheeks, chronic bad breath, damaged teeth, or calluses on their knuckles (side effects caused by induced vomiting)
- ongoing stomach issues such as cramps, acid reflux, and constipation
- cracked or thin nails and skin
- thinning/loss of hair
- fine hair growth on body
- blotchy/spotty purplish hands/feet that are cold to the touch

**Medical Signs:**
- blood work may reveal anemia
- low hormone or thyroid levels
- wounds that take a long time to heal

**Behavioral Signs:**
- counting calories
- elimination dieting (cutting out entire food groups)
- identifying "good" and "bad" foods
- fasting
- visiting the bathroom during or immediately after finishing a meal
- controlling portion sizes
- rigidity in foods they consume
- avoiding foods they used to love

- vomiting
- restricting socializing so that it doesn't fall around mealtimes
- becoming secretive about their eating, saying they've already eaten, or wanting to eat alone
- sensitivity and defensiveness about comments regarding their weight, their exercise schedules, or their eating habits
- increased/excessive exercise (including exercising while injured or exercising multiple times in a day)
- exclusively wearing oversized clothes

**Psychological Signs:**
- demonstrating a strong need to be in control but having a sense of being out of control around food
- having an unrealistic/distorted image of their body
- behaving anxious or irritable around mealtimes
- obsessing over food and eating
- using food as a punishment or comfort
- being consumed with their weight and exercise[9]

This list can be super scary, and my best advice to you is that you do everything you can to ensure that an ED doesn't come into your home in the first place. Now, as your new friend, I'm going to say something, and I don't want you to get mad at me because I'm well aware that EDs are mental health issues, but you also need to consider your kid's environmental surroundings. Think about what they hear. What they see. What they're taught. Think about the times you've talked about your weight, about how your clothes don't fit the same, about how you need to diet, or about how you can't eat that sweet because it's bad for you. All the things we're all guilty of saying, without realizing what we're saying, can be triggering one of our kids who is predisposed to develop an eating disorder. Casual, harmless conversations about food could be playing a massive role in bringing to the surface ED urges in a child who may be, like me, ripe for the picking. And not necessarily because they were sexually abused—not all kids who develop eating disorders have been. Our daughter wasn't. And not necessarily because they were raised by a neglectful, drunk father. Sometimes all it takes is the wrong language over and over and over again, or consistent casual and (what we deem) harmless conversations around food that could be playing a massive role in bringing to the surface disordered eating in a vulnerable teen.

> The best way to be a good parent is to be a humble one.

I'm sure it is never intentional that a parent aid in festering an ED by having innocuous conversations, something I believe because I'm guilty of it too. The number of juice cleanses I've done after the holidays? Too many to count. The list of times I've complained about my back boobs with my girls in earshot? Holy fuck, it's shamefully way too long. I'm not calling the kettle black here, friends, I am in the fire with you. I, too, have accidentally, unwittingly passed my disordered relationship to food down onto my girls. I consistently participated in negative self-talk about my body and about what I was or wasn't eating, and I had a daughter pay the price, which is why I'm driving home the point with you to become informed before an eating disorder moves in with you and your beautiful kid(s).

No matter the age of your child, it's not too early to become familiar with EDs or to start a dialogue with them about food. Use these questions as a guide:

- Do they ever eat anything and feel guilty about what they've had?
- Do they believe that there are good and bad foods?
- Do they have friends who call themselves fat?
- Have they ever called themselves fat?

Then do the really hard part of having the dialogue about food with your kid. Ask them questions about you and your relationship to food and their interpretation of it. They may not feel comfortable at first speaking truthfully about how your food habits have affected them, especially if, like me, you have unconsciously been sending them negative signals about food. And their answers may sting a bit.

I said it in my first book, and I've said here: The best way to be a good parent is to be a humble one. Your children aren't out to get you. They love you. They think you're the greatest human on the planet, but when you reach out to them to get their honest input as to how you can be a better caregiver and teacher for them, do them a favor and listen with your heart, not your ego. Their development into humans who can grow into people who can have constructive and difficult conversations with other key relationships in their lives all begins at home, with you. With you giving them the space to speak their truth respectfully, in the safe bubble of your love.

The bottom line here, parents, is not to shame, guilt, or upset you, or call you a bad parent. The truth is, if you're a human being, you've fucked up with your kid a time or two about food. And that's okay. We don't know what we don't know. The great news is that everything we've done to our kids, by the grace of God, can be undone. And now that you're aware as to the possible side effects speaking negatively about food can have on your beautiful, pure, and innocent kids, it's time to cut off this behavior immediately. Should your child(ren) already be showing signs of developing, or having one or more disordered-eating behaviors brewing, seek immediate professional help. My mom didn't have the means to get me the help I needed, and honestly, I didn't even know up until doing research for this part of this book that my eating disorder is still alive and well in me too, so let's just say this girl is going back to the well of well-being by getting some help with somebody who specializes in healing eating disorders, pronto. It's never too late to seek help, so whoever is reading these words right now, if you feel like you can see yourself in this section of the book, and you believe you might have an ED of your own, this is your chance to get the aid you need to heal this disorder within yourself too by also seeking professional help.

Damn!

Wow. This is a heavy chapter, isn't it? I feel like it should come with an apology, but if I did, I'd be perpetuating the stigma around not talking about all the dark corners of raising a teen—the dark corners that my girlfriends and I didn't talk about and didn't help one another through because we were too embarrassed, ashamed, and scared to even discuss them! We truly thought that we were the only parent having these challenges with our kids, and had we only put our egos aside, we could have provided a tremendous amount of comfort to each other during the difficult and dark days. On those days when you feel like you're going through something that is too overwhelming and heavy, let this book be a safe space for you to land. Or message me directly. Nobody needs to go it alone. It is so common as a parent to think that we are the only one experiencing these challenges with our kids, but the truth is, we aren't. I'm not here to freak you out; I'm here to be as honest with you as is humanly possible. I'm here to present you with all the potential scenarios you might find yourself in with your teen. Of course, what's in this book is my truth from my personal experience, and your parenting journey might not ever include a fraction of what I experienced as a mom, but just in case it does, I'm going to put it all in here for you, which leads me to our next topic, another doozy, but a very real crisis that so many teens face.

## SELF-HARM

I'll never forget being in the ninth grade. It had been another day of having my locker "Coked" (when somebody pours Coca-Cola through the slats of your locker door and it gets all over your stuff . . . it is about as messy and shitty as it sounds) and wiping the word SLUT from the outside of it. When I finally made it home to my room, I fell onto my bed and sobbed. I was distressed and confused and totally bewildered as to why someone would do something so awful to somebody for no reason. I don't know how or why it happened, but I suddenly started to claw at my face with my fingernails. I don't know where the urge to harm myself came from, I just recall thinking, "Maybe if I'm ugly, they will all just leave me alone."

And in that moment, the only thing that mattered to me in the world was to be left alone. That was all I wanted. Luckily, my nails were short, and I didn't break the skin, but my face was raw and puffy from my attempt to soothe myself / change my appearance to stop the bullying of raging bitches who were shitty humans. I'm grateful every day that I didn't end up scarring myself for life at the hands at a group of girls who mattered less than nothing in the grand scheme of my incredible life.

I was one of the lucky ones.

Your child might not get so lucky.

First things first. The intent of self-harm is rarely suicide. Suicidal tendencies are a whole other batch of desperate calls for help to relieve the disproportionate amount of pain that a person is in. If you have a child who is suicidal, circle the wagons immediately. If any of our girls had ever gotten to the point where they were displaying suicidal tendencies, Yannick and I had a plan—we would place them into protective medical care at once. We had decided that in that area, we would not play the "wait and see" game. I think we also got extremely lucky that we had a rather large village around our girls: some were family members, but others were friends we deeply admired, loved, and trusted. We would call on them and bring them in close when the girls were going through their dark and scary days/months/years. We always knew that we couldn't save them on our own. I suggest that you start building your village now if you don't already have one. It's never too late to have somebody outside of you and your partner to take them to the movies, on hikes, shopping . . . whatever it is your tween/teen loves to do. Pull others in. Let them play a role in ensuring the mental wellness of your child.

Promise me that if you have a child who you believe is leaning toward suicide that you don't wait to see if you're overreacting. Get help. And remember, if your kid is self-harming, just because the statistics say that it's not a precursor to suicide, don't hesitate to get your kid the help and support they need. It is not the time to be an ostrich parent; you're not raising a baby ostrich. You're raising a human being, so be present, even though it's hard, painful, and scary when it feels like there is no end in sight to their pain and suffering. But trust me, I have great faith in your strength and the strength of your teen. If you get them qualified help, you will save them from these dark, tumultuous times. This is not a time to allow your ego to take the lead, to start to worry about things like "Well, what if the Joneses find out our kid is on medication, or has been committed . . ." Who cares about anybody else if/when your child is in a crisis? Drop the façade and get into the trenches with your kid—it will probably save their life.

Start building your village now if you don't already have one.

It's extremely important that we start to connect the dots with our teens. Because as you can see now that we're deep into the teen life, one thing often leads to another, to another, to another. They don't just wake up depressed one day. Or start self-harming. Or with the urge to stop eating. Typically, these behaviors coexist with each other. The American Psychological Association has stated that there is a strong link between depression and self-injury.[10] Although the thought of your beautiful child that you love so much injuring themselves is terrifying, you must know that self-injury is almost always impulsive and not intended to be lethal. And if your teen does suffer from depression, it doesn't always mean they will go on to self-harm, which is a massive relief. But this is not break time for you; it is still your job to be on top of all the things your teen is dealing with. And nobody appreciates more than I do what a huge undertaking being on top of more than one teen is! Don't leave them to deal with it on their own; you are the captain of their ship, they're the co-captain. Remember that. They don't know where they're going or what they're dealing with or how to recover from never-ending bullshit at school—you need to support and guide them through all the muck.

Ask the questions. Be aware, and a great way to be aware is by being armed with knowledge, which I can help you with. Here's a list of self-harming signs to look out for:

- skin cutting
- head banging
- hitting themselves
- skin burning
- excessive scratching to the point of drawing blood
- ingesting harmful substances
- inserting foreign objects into body cavities
- breaking bones purposely

Often, people who self-harm attempt to hide their marks with long sleeves and pants. If your teen suddenly begins covering their body when they didn't before, or in hot weather, get involved. And please, if you discover that your child is self-harming (or even just suspect it), step in. Book them in for a physical examination with their doctor so their doctor can conduct a medical evaluation. If you have the sort of relationship with your teen, which I hope you do, where you're able to speak with them about your suspicions/concerns for their well-being, and you believe that you'll be able to have a truthful and constructive conversation with them, then go that route first. But if you know your child is suffering, and they're presenting some of these warning signs and you want to get a professional involved right away, well, then do that. Do whatever feels best for your parental instinct, aka your gut, and get the help. Now. Don't hesitate. The emphatic call to never hesitate to get help when you're out of your depth as a parent takes us into the final topic of this chapter.

## GENDER IDENTITY STRUGGLES

What a beautiful time we live in. Our world is evolving. Yes, there are many people who are fighting change tooth and nail, attempting to hold on to antiquated ways of seeing and treating others, but for the most part, the instances of tolerance and acceptance are growing. And to that I say, hallelujah and AMEN because now kids who don't identify as the gender they were born with have hope—hope that they, too, can live as freely as those who fully identify as female if born female or male when born male. It is a gift as a parent to be able to embrace your child for who they truly are. I know nothing about raising a transgender human, but I do know a thing or two about raising teens, and those years can be so difficult for a kid to navigate that I can only imagine that it cannot be at all easy for our transgender youth. Yes, our world has made leaps and bounds in becoming more tolerant of differences, but we're not quite there yet the globe over. There still is so much discrimination and fear that comes from people who don't understand.

To these people I say, "It's none of your business what gender somebody identifies as. Like, what the hell difference does it make over your Sunday dinner or in your household if somebody else was born male but identifies as female?" The reality is that the only person gender should matter to is the person who doesn't identify with the one they were assigned at birth.

Everybody else, mind your business.

To the parents of a child who comes forward (and *bravely* I might add because honestly, that requires some serious strength), I commend you for the steadfast love, support, and strength that I know you're giving your teen. Good for you. You are superhero parents, and I sincerely mean that with my entire heart. You're the real MVPs, and your kids are so lucky to have you in their corner. As a parent, one thing I know for certain is that like me, you have been living with your heart outside of your body ever since your child entered your life, and now you have this added worry about how the world will treat them after they've come out . . . it can't be easy. It must be incredibly lonely and isolating. And because I have no experience in this parenting reality that you are in, I will do as I have learned to do: I will refrain from commenting on what I think you should do because I legitimately have no clue. But I will do what I would do if we were in-person friends and you shared with me that your child (who I would obviously be madly in love with too!) has recently told you about their gender identification.

I would start by acknowledging what it is you're going through by honoring your feelings. "I'm so sorry that you are going through this tough time. It must be so destabilizing. You must feel out of your depth and be completely at a loss as to where you go from here." Then I would let you know that I was with you, that I have your back, and that I believe in you: "I just want you to know that I know how much you love your baby, and I know that if anybody can figure how to guide them through this with confidence and all the support in the world, it is you."

Then I would likely ask you whether your child is completely certain that they are, in fact, not the gender they were assigned at birth. And if they're certain, then I would advise you to get reading and to get following positive role models on the internet, like Gabrielle Union and Cher, who could help you to feel supported in this new, unchartered territory of your parenting journey.

As for reading, Johns Hopkins has a lot of transgender and gender fluid book recommendations for children, teens, and parents on their website.[11] Additionally, Stephanie A. Brill and Lisa Kinney have an excellent book called *The Transgender Teen: A Handbook for Parents and Professionals Supporting Transgender and Non-Binary Teens.* There are some great resources out there, folks, so I encourage you to find ones that help you through this time.

The bottom line is that it won't be an easy journey for you or your teen. But the more you know, the more you know, so educate yourself. Find a fantastic therapist or psychologist who specializes in supporting kids and parents alike in the transition. You must not try to go it alone. And for the love of God, don't try to sweep it under the rug or keep it undercover. That never ends well. Make sure you join a support group, online or in person, so you can get help from other parents who are living it!

Also . . . be real. Make sure you have a solid group of ride-or-dies who you can turn to with the new information you'll be given during the coming-to-terms days/weeks/months ahead—people with whom you can share all your thoughts (good, bad, or ugly) without censoring yourself and who you trust to take your secrets to their graves. Because yes, it will be difficult for your kid to come out into the world as their true self, but let's be blunt here and acknowledge that it likely won't be a walk in the park for you parents either, initially. But with time, and the proper support around you, I believe in the end it will all be okay. Hell, it will be better than okay because you'll be helping your beloved bold, fierce child live life as who they truly are. And I don't need to tell you that your kid gets one life, so it's up to you to make sure that it's a fucking awesome one!

And you, my friend, are doing a kick-ass job at it, so I salute you! You've got this.

## Things to Nibble On

♡ What a heavy chapter. So, I'm going to keep this wrap-up as brief as possible. For sure, your kid is going to lie, and they will do it more times than you bargained for. And here's the thing about lying: If you let it slide, even when you know they're lying, they'll only lie more because they'll think they're getting away with it. Nip this behavior in the bud right away. Nobody likes a liar. Nobody.

♡ It may just seem like your teen is having trouble with hormones and all their growing pains and, you know, spending a lot of time in their room alone, chilling, FaceTiming, and Snapchatting their lives away, but if there is a family history of depression or mental health issues, get involved; start asking your child how they're **really** doing. Remember, it's always recommended to get your kid help sooner rather than later.

♡ It can be hard to recognize disordered-eating patterns in your kid's life given how a lot of us have spent the better part of our lives on diets. Look for the signs, ask the questions, be involved. Get help.

♡ I included all these topics in one chapter because they tend to coexist with each other. Where you find one, you often find another. I cannot stress it enough: Pay very close attention to your teen. They can self-harm extremely quietly and under the radar. Know the signs and look for them. And if you see them, don't hesitate to GET THEM HELP!

♡ For those of you who have a teen who is struggling with gender identity, be brave enough to allow them the freedom to be who they truly are. Have a coach or expert in your corner, and love, love, love that child of yours. Your unconditional love is so vital, and I wish you all peace in your new normal as a family. May the entire world catch up to your evolvement.

♡ I'd tell you to go have sex, but I'm going to give you a break because this chapter had A LOT to take in. Perhaps you're feeling more like you could use a few shots of whiskey and a week in bed. You do whatever you need to do, and I'll see you on the other side!

# Chapter Eight

# EDUCATION AND PROBLEM-SOLVING

I know. That last chapter was an eye-opening one. We tackled a whole pile of the difficult, scary, shocking parts of being baptized into the fire of parenting teens. Some of the topics you may be familiar with personally, or perhaps you've witnessed friends, classmates, colleagues, whomever, go through them. It is my prayer that by reading the last chapter you feel confident knowing that while you may cross one or more of those bridges, you will be OKAY. Why? Because you will call in some backup, get professional help when needed, and most of all, you will be patient with yourself, your teen, and your partner, and you will not go through it alone. Because, hey—it's all new to all of you, and freaking out, shutting down, or running away won't change the fact that you're here now. This life with your teen is your new reality, so the best thing to do for everybody involved is to put your big-girl/big-boy pants on and get it done. Be the supportive, loving, under-standing parent your teen needs you to be. They'll thank you for it, because once you accept them for who they are, you open them up to the ability to become fully formed. When they don't have the pressure of maintaining perfection in your eyes, they can be authentic with you and themselves. And this inner freedom and their complete trust in you will allow them to feel stronger about your relationship with them because they know you've got their back!

By now I think it's pretty obvious that I'm all about love and support, but make sure you have some healthy boundaries and that you keep your cool. Don't start handling your child with kid gloves or get all up in their business for no reason. Don't take your PTA involvement to a fevered pitch! Don't let your worry over the wellness of your child cause you to lose your mind! Don't get over involved in their school lives while you try to take care of their emotional/mental ones. You still need to leave them some room to breathe. The bottom line here is that your kid's middle and high school years are not a chance for you to relive your youth. To do it better. To do that science fair project you've always wanted to do or whatever the hell it is you wish you could go back and do over. It is their time. Their experiences. Their chance to grow and evolve into their own people.

Give them some damn space and allow them to hit some bumps in the road along the way. Stop doing their homework if you're still helping with it. Stop calling/emailing/challenging teachers because your child feels like they didn't get the grade they deserved. I mean, I have never seen somebody sitting at their office desk with their mom sitting beside them, nor have I ever seen a kid in a lecture hall with their dad taking their notes.

Give them some room to figure it out on their own. And then if they can't, or if they have learning challenges, then you step in. I'm not telling you to ignore extraordinary situations. If your child needs your help on an ongoing basis, you give it. This is not a book on how to neglect your child. But if you have a kid who is perfectly capable of complaining incessantly about a grade over breakfast, lunch, and dinner, then teach that child how to approach their teacher and talk about it. Teach them to be respectfully bold and to plead their case if they feel like they've not received the grade they worked hard to earn. But they do it, not *you.*

Right now, you might be thinking, "Wow, you're a cold-hearted bitch, Shantelle, and you don't know my kid who has so-and-so disorder, so I must help them."

I thought I was pretty clear above but let me expand my thoughts here. a) I apologize for not knowing this information about your kid, and b) if this is your family's reality, then obviously your teen will need your help/support with doing their work, and you'll need to have open correspondence with their teachers. And that's FINE. I'm not talking about extenuating circumstances, I'm referring to the busybody parents, *you know who you are,* who are too deep into their kids' education in all the not-helpful ways.

So, if you are one of these parents, here are some helpful tips to get your kid learning on their own two feet. Because regardless of the age of your child, these hard-and-fast rules still apply, IMO.

## LETTING THEM WORK OUT THEIR OWN SCHOOL LIFE

Listen, here's the skinny on schoolteachers and projects. You and I both know that if your kid neglects to hand in their assignment by the due date, they are going to lose marks. And the chances of a teacher giving your precious child any extra time to get the project done are slim to none. Similarly, when they head out into the grown-up world of working, a boss isn't going to keep them around for very long if

> Your kid's middle and high school years are not a chance for you to relive your youth.
>
> ♡

they throw a tantrum every single time they're asked to perform their duties—duties they are paid to do. I think you and I can both agree on these points. I mean, neither of us is new here.

Let me let you in on the biggest parenting secret: It is not your job to do your kid's homework or their projects. Their elementary/middle/ high school days aren't your chance to relive/redo it all! This is your kid's one life. You've gotta let them live it—the good, the bad, the ugly—all of it. Letting them go out into the deep end allows them to learn problem-solving skills. Encourage them go back to their teacher and seek extra help. Allow them to experience life without you holding their hand and fighting their battles. You're not always going to be around, so make sure you give them what they need to succeed, and one of the best ways to give them that is by teaching them to trust in their own ability to make it to the other side of a challenging situation by finding the solution themselves.

Removing all the difficulties out of your children's lives, clearing the way of any and all hardships, will result in the opposite outcome of what I believe you want. Treating them this way is definitely not going to create strong, resilient adults. Your teen may feel better in the moment with your safety net there to catch them, or never knowing struggle. But what do you think happens when they go out into the world on their own? When they go out into the world, and their teacher or their boss challenges them on where their homework is or why they didn't get their part of a contract completed on time, they need to be able to accept responsibility for their choices, and they can't if you're all in the mix. Be supportive, be a help to them, but don't *live their lives for them*. Remember, this book is to teach you *long-game* mentality. You will make a more confident, problem-solving human as a result. You will all have fuller, richer lives, and you will be proud as you watch them come into their own, knowing that you didn't hand it to them, you merely guided them along the way.

## HOLD THEM ACCOUNTABLE FOR THEIR CHOICES

This topic is another favorite one of mine that I've been witnessing with some parents out in the wild—the lack of willingness to either believe their kids could ever treat anybody poorly, or once they realize that their child can be an asshole, and has the receipts presented to them that they *were*, in fact, a complete and utter asshole, they still don't hold their mini-them accountable for their choices. I think one of the most disgusting, blatant examples of this type of parent was showcased during the Brock Turner fiasco, when his loser father said the now infamous words about his son's sentence for sexual assault: "[The sentence] is a steep price to pay for twenty minutes of action out of his twenty plus years of life."

Disgusting.

Open communication is crucial in establishing your relationship with your teen, so when they behave in a way that goes against your rules/expectations for their conduct, you have the foundation to back you up while throwing down the consequence. They will never take responsibility for dropping the ball in their own lives if you don't teach them how to accept responsibility for it in their own home. One part of our role as parents is to have ongoing frank, open, honest dialogues with our kids. We need to know them. Like really know them, and not just on family vacations or through their social media. We need to be *in their lives* every day, and a great way to spend time together is to sit down and have a meal as a family. Our family set the goal of having at least one of our meals together every day. If somebody was going to be home late at night from work or from extracurricular activities, then we made sure to eat together in the morning before everybody left for their days.

During these meals, we played games like High-Low, where each person shared the best part of their day and their low point, sparking conversation about what about it was so difficult, how we handled it, and how we could find a way to feel better about the situation. We did the same thing when talking about the high points. It's called communication—you know, that crucial thing I keep bringing up?

> It is super important to have a solid foundation of communication with your teen.

I know, I know. I'm like a broken record about this, but it is super important to have a solid foundation of communication with your teen. You need to be asking them questions and to be listening between the lines, so you are always aware of what's going on. You're *inside* their lives, and through dialogue, you learn so much about them and their daily lives, like whether they take responsibility for their actions when they're out in the wild. You don't want your kids to become "buck-passers."

If you own a company, or if you've ever worked as part of a team, I'm sure you've encountered someone who doesn't take ownership for their part—the person who loves to "pass the buck" of blame onto somebody else, who has zero humility, and who won't accept responsibility when they drop the ball.

Now, can we all take a moment to consider how we feel about these kinds of people? Are these the people you want to have over for dinner?

No.

No, you do not want to chill with these people. You want to wring their necks.

Now, let me ask you this question: Is this the kind of person you want to put out into the world? Think about your beautiful, wonderful, amazing child, the teen you've spent so many years investing time, energy, and integrity into raising—one of the only people you would lay down your life for. Do you want them to become one of these people?

No, you do not.

So, do the work, and a large part of that work is letting them fail. You also want to hold their hand to the fire when they behave like total and absolute jerks out in the world. Parenting is all about balance, my friends, and it's about leading by example. One way kids learn to accept responsibility in their lives is when they witness their parents have it in their own. So, make sure they see you admit when you blow it, take ownership, and apologize to the people you need to apologize to while they bear witness. Sometimes, in my experience, I've found with my own girls that it was my actions that taught them the greatest lessons in becoming good humans!

### Things to Nibble On

♡ Love them enough to help them just enough. Don't be there ever ready with the safety net so they never learn what it feels like to hit the bottom. Either you let them do it while they live under your roof and the lesson is taught to them in safety, or you shelter them so much that they never know how to stand up under the weight of disappointment only to learn it once they get out in the real world. Either way, they will receive the lesson.

♡ Make sure you hold your kid accountable for their choices. Nobody likes a buck-passer, so be diligent in holding your child responsible for any asshole behavior that you witness or get informed about. You owe it to their future lovers, friends, and co-workers to raise them to be the sort of person who can say, "I'm sorry" or "I fucked up."

♡ I didn't mention it because by now I'd hope that it's a given, so don't let me down. Remember to keep your intimate relationship with your partner front and center. The kids leave, or at least they're supposed to, and you want to be sure that you and your co-parent still know and love each other. So, stay connected, however that looks for you. Perhaps, like me, you allow your person to throw you down a mountain, either on skis or a mountain bike. Whatever it is, stay close so you can keep on having that sex! And if you're footloose and fancy-free, then dare I say that the world of pleasure is your oyster!

# Chapter Nine

# SOCIAL MEDIA AND CATFISHING

I did you a solid and lightened the continuation of your parenting education with a short and pretty straightforward, digestible chapter. Now that we've ticked off holding teens accountable and letting them learn tough lessons, it's time to let them do hard things, as Glennon Doyle has famously said. Your teen can do it! And much of the reason why is thanks to you giving them the space to learn how truly smart, resilient, and resourceful they are. By allowing your kids to get themselves backed into a corner based on decisions/choices they've made and then allowing them the space to work themselves out of it, you're showing them that you believe in them and trust them to fix their mess without your involvement. Your confidence in them breeds more confidence within themselves. As you witness them killing the game and growing into a strong, bold, empowered person, you cheer them on even harder, getting them more fired up and pushing them to grow even more . . . and it goes on and on and on and on.

So, now that we're celebrating the victory that is your teen fighting their own battles and learning how to be grown-ups, let's make sure that we're not letting them get too grown up in the wrong ways.

"What are you talking about, Shantelle? You're talking out of both sides of your face."

I'm talking about social media.

My humble opinion, as I witness friends battle this demon now with their tweens, is that if you haven't already done so, which for the love of God I really hope you have, set strong boundaries around social media. This rule is not about you being a giant asshole. Your child may argue that Vicki's mom lets her sleep with her phone and have a boyfriend at age ten plus have Instagram and TikTok accounts that her parents aren't allowed to follow or have the password for, but that's going to be a big no for you. It's your house, your rules, and you don't play by Vicki's parents' rules. Don't buy into it. Let me assure you, as I know from what my girls share with me and what girlfriends with young kids have told me, the creeps are out there. Sliding into DMs daily. Sending dick pics. Trying to entice your precious child into sending nudes for money. Monitor your kids' online lives by having their passwords; it's for their own good. Let me tell you that for as much good that happens online, and you really hope that Jacob and Susie are only looking at puppy videos, there is a whole whack of no good taking place on the internet. Trust a woman who works with an organization in Toronto called Boost for Kids, which assists kids in charging their predators and overcoming the trauma of sexual abuse, when she tells you that the number of online predators is MASSIVE. The information I have gained from working with this organization, combined with daily conversations with my three adult daughters, has me staying in the know of how often they and all their friends get approached via DMs on their social media to get paid to send photos of themselves for money.

And if this isn't enough to get you to rethink your casual attitude toward social media, maybe you'll take it from a friend of mine who works in internet security. What we see all day long on the internet and social media is literally the tip of the dark, seedy, underbelly of what is really going on out there. He knows some SHIT that would curl your toes and have you crying, "Mommy!"

So, please, please, please trust me and all of us who have gone before you! If you think you don't need to teach them about social media or have access to their accounts if they're under the age of sixteen, think again. Take off your rose-colored glasses, come into the land of online predatory life, and do your job. Slay those predatory demons and protect your kids no matter how much they bargain to have unsupervised online freedom. Be willing to be "such an asshole" in order to keep them safe. If your kid is suddenly showing up with designer sneakers/handbags/clothes (that you did not buy them and they don't have a part-time job to pay for), start asking questions—lots and lots and lots of questions. And if you haven't read the book *Protecting the Gift* by Gavin de Becker, run out and get it! It was and still is one of the top five parenting books I've ever read. You only get one chance to protect your kids, and you must take it; they are counting on you to do so.

Since we adults know the very dark/twisted/negative sides of online living, let's set up healthy boundaries for what social media is going to look like in your family's home. We will work it out together.

## WHAT'S A GOOD AGE TO ALLOW MY KID TO HAVE SOCIAL MEDIA?

If I sold a book for every single time I get asked this question, I'd be a *New York Times* best-selling author! But alas, I give my advice for free when people ask me because I'm so passionate about the negative mental impact that social media has on the developing brain of adolescents. And now I'll give it to you here.

I am so happy that most social media platforms didn't come around until my girls were already formed. It's interesting to hear my adult girls talk about social media. They know it's full of completely fake, manufactured highlight reels of other people's lives, yet they still aspire to have similar lives to those they see online. They know they're being manipulated by the platforms to see certain things. I mean, Facebook famously conducted an experiment using 700,000 of their users without their knowledge. They fed certain users only negative, upsetting content, others neutral content, and then still others only positive, upbeat stuff to see how it affected their posts. Would these images change the users' personalities / mental states? The users had no idea that their feeds were being manipulated in this way. Meanwhile, Facebook watched the psychological fallout: Does constant negative commentary and imagery create a negative reaction in otherwise emotionally balanced people? You can imagine the havoc this experiment made on people with preexisting issues of mental illness. Yup. That's a thing that happened. Google it.

How about you do a little science experiment of your own, with yourself as the subject? Keep a journal of your social media use. For one week, spend as much time as is available to you on social media. Go on every platform you follow: Twitter, Facebook, Instagram, etc. Spend as much time as you can shake loose, then take stock of how you feel after that week. How is your mood? How do you feel about yourself? Your station in life? Your career? All of it. All the things. The most important key to this self-experiment is that you have to be brutally honest with yourself about how the excessive time made you feel.

Once you're done, consider your child's emotional/mental

development and maturity level and deduce for yourself what age is appropriate for them to be on social media. Because I have to tell you, those influencers and people out there who have a bajillion followers for doing things like, you know, pouting, or mimicking other people, or opening gifts that get sent to them, these people are "famous" to your kids. And the reality is that just because your kid jumps on there and talks into their phone about, well, nothing at all, doesn't mean their follower count is going to go through the roof or that Prada is going to send them shoes and handbags. So, since you and I both know this isn't likely to be their reality, then how about we shelter them a little bit longer? Because you want to know what I can *guarantee* is going to happen the second they get on social media?

**A sugar daddy will appear.**

Your kid is 1,000,000 percent going to get approached by some strange weirdo pervert to become their sugar baby. Don't believe me? Let's take a look how some Canadian universities rank in the Sugar Baby World:[12]

## CANADA:

| RANK | UNIVERSITY | STUDENT MEMBERS |
|------|------------|-----------------|
| 1 | University of Toronto | 257 |
| 2 | University of Alberta | 231 |
| 3 | Queens University | 222 |
| 4 | Ryerson University | 179 |
| 5 | Wilfred Laurier University | 145 |
| 6 | York University | 141 |
| 7 | University of Guelph | 139 |
| 8 | Dalhousie University | 109 |
| 9 | McGill University | 108 |
| 10 | Mount Royal University | 104 |

Yikes, right?!

And let's not leave out our US counterpart. It's a big country, and postsecondary tuition is crazy expensive. The largest driving force behind kids getting themselves into this type of situation is debt, so it stands to reason that there are plenty of sugar babies in the US university school system:[13]

| RANK | UNIVERSITY | STUDENT MEMBERS |
|------|-----------|-----------------|
| 1 | Arizona State | 2,680 |
| 2 | Indiana State | 1,286 |
| 3 | University of Central Florida | 1,142 |
| 4 | New York University | 1,115 |
| 5 | University of Wisconsin | 1,061 |
| 6 | University of Arizona | 1,054 |
| 7 | Florida International University | 1,042 |
| 8 | University of Texas | 980 |
| 9 | University of Illinois | 965 |
| 10 | Kent State University | 964 |
| 11 | University of Colorado | 952 |
| 12 | University of South Florida | 948 |
| 13 | University of Alabama | 945 |
| 14 | Ohio State University | 939 |

Being a sugar baby is a very real thing, and the men who want a sugar baby but don't want to register on a site know that the demand for their "gifts" is out there. They are trolling. And they are sliding into your teens DMs all day, every day. I don't know one girl who my daughters are friends with who have *not* been approached multiple times. So, I ask you, are you prepared for your ten, eleven, twelve or thirteen-year-old to be dealing with being propositioned? My girls are adults, and I'm totally bothered by it every single time they tell me about another "hit" to their account. But I was even more bothered when a good girlfriend of mine told me years ago that her then ten-year-old was DMed by a man who said he thought she was beautiful and wondered if she would like to shave his balls.

Yes.

This stuff is going on out there, people.

Horrifying.

Now, I know that I've been talking about female sugar babies here, but what you need to understand is that this sexual solicitation is not biased about gender. Parents of boys, don't think you're getting off scot-free, because you're not. Your son probably has a story or two of a woman or gay man wanting a piece of them too. Nobody is safe on these platforms. Check out these numbers from the US as of April 2021:[14]

| Sugar Babies (F) | Sugar Babies (M) | Sugar Daddies | Sugar Mamas |
|---|---|---|---|
| **8,772,014** | **3,278,736** | **2,101,359** | **370,498** |

Wow, right!

It's a wild, *wild* world out there, my friends. I've said it before, and I'll say it again: I'm not here to freak you out or drive you to drink (although I honestly wouldn't blame you if you started now—the timeline adds up). I'm here to open your eyes to what is going on in the world around you and around your kid so you can be prepared for it. You can't win a war you don't know you're fighting, and since some of you may not yet have a kid in the teen years, you're probably not even thinking about this sort of shit coming your way. But you must know, if you're going to allow your child to be on these platforms, then you absolutely

> You need to instruct your kids about being private on social media.

have to tell them that the only way you're going to allow it is by you having access to their account. You need to instruct them about being private—they can't hashtag their photos or have locations on anything, especially their photos. Any way that anybody can potentially come in their back door needs to be on lockdown.

Do we have a deal?

Now that we're having so much fun discussing the seedy underbelly of social media, let me let you in on another little secret about what your teen has to look forward to online.

## CATFISHING AND ONLINE IDENTITY THEFT

Chances are you know a little bit about these things because there's a TV show out there that deals with this exact topic, and when you're watching it on TV, it's sort of funny. Or you may be watching and thinking, "How does this happen to people? How do they get taken for a ride in this way?" Well, it's simple. People are lonely—they're craving human connection, for starters. People want to feel loved, desirable, special, and valued. And vulnerable people get preyed upon. It's sad, disgusting, and wrong. Remember my friend I told you about earlier who's in internet security, as in securing the internet for some agencies with mega high security? He loves to say, "If only the people who hack into people's accounts would use their skills for good instead of evil, the world would be a much better place." And I have to say, I can't agree more.

So, another risk your child might encounter out there in the adult world of social media is having their accounts stolen for porn sites.

Yup.

THE FUCK, right?!

Child porn sites.

Adult porn sites.

You name it. Your kid's innocent beach photos of building a sand castle, or standing with the fish they just caught, or surfing in their cute little swimsuit . . . you guessed it—stolen and luring sickos to child pornography sites.

And if your kid is a teen posing with friends or alone at the pool, beach, wherever, those are up for grabs too!

How do I know? Well, I know because it happened to one of my daughters. I know because we lived it, as have way too many of my daughters' friends. I haven't had any of my friends tell me that it's happened to their sons, but my guess is that it probably has.

Look, I'm not here to make you paranoid. I'm really not. I'm giving you knowledge so you can do everything you can to protect your child. Perhaps it's never happened to you or your kid, so you think somebody like me saying, "Keep your kid off social media until they're at least sixteen" is because I'm a dick and no fun. Not at all. I'm giving you my advice so you can protect them for as long as you can. It is bananas out there. And I would hope that you're glad someone is educating you on the part of social media that you're not privy to, since it would be my guess that nobody is sliding into your DMs asking you to be their sugar baby. And it's not because you're not hot or sexy because I'm sure you totally are. It's because you're not significantly younger than the old perverts who are looking for sugar babies, or posting bathing suit shots, or alluding to the fact that you are single and in debt.

I recommend that you encourage and champion your kid to have a part-time job as soon as they can. The combination of them being financially sound (or as sound as one can be while they're a student) and knowing that you are aware that this seedy world exists will help in keeping them from falling prey to the "harmless" temptations of selling photos of their feet, their ass, their breasts, their lips sucking a cucumber . . . you name it. And if your kid comes at you all mad and upset that you're insisting on having access to their online social lives, well, you can either stand firm and keep them off it until they agree to follow the rules you established, or you can cave and trust them to behave out there in the wild on their own.

Making this decision is where having the unity of your parenting partner, if you have one, is paramount. You must both be on the same side of the fence. A united front is much harder for your teen to defeat. So, stand firm. Stand firm in the conviction that your rules are for their own good and safety. Let your word be law when it comes to their social media access.

And before we leave this chapter, I have to say that it's super important that you also have some hard-and-fast rules about device usage.

What do I mean?

Well, for example, there shouldn't be any devices at the table during mealtimes. Any mealtimes. I totally believe that young ones should not have their phones in their bedrooms. Have a cabinet where their devices go after a certain time to ensure your kiddos are getting proper sleep. Tired people don't cope well with stress and they also have trouble concentrating and don't do as well in school. And I definitely recommend that you don't allow your kids to have their devices with them while they're doing homework. In our house, homework was done at the dining room table. This way I made sure my girls got it done in a timely fashion, rather than wasting time up in their rooms doing Lord knows what.

Give your kid an allotted time period when they can be on their device. Perhaps in your house it works best for your kid to come

Let your word be law when it comes to their social media access.

home, unwind, have a snack, get on their device for an hour, then tuck into homework before dinner. Or maybe you have the sort of kid who prefers to stay in the school groove so gets down to business right away, leaving device time for before or after dinner. It's for you to decide. But whatever you do determine is best for your household and your child, I will strongly suggest that you don't allow them access to it right before bed. The blue light interferes with the part of the brain that prepares for sleep. And as we touched upon earlier, the emotional/mental stressors of watching everybody's highlight reel wreaks havoc on their mental well-being right before sleep, which is super counter-intuitive for a good night's rest!

So, once you've won this war, slide into bed and get busy. Remember: Being sexy isn't an age thing, it's a mindset. And you've still got it, baby!

## Things to Nibble On

♡ Nobody knows your child(ren) better than you. Only you know what they can emotionally and mentally handle. You're the best judge of their ability to withstand all that is social media.

♡ You're not going to bury your head in the sand like an ostrich. You now know about the super active role of sugar daddies on the internet, and you are going to ask the real and tough questions about your teen's online activities. And if they're under sixteen, you will be inside their social media because you have access to their accounts. By the way, lots of nudes are sent via Snapchat, so make sure you have access to that account too!

♡ There is an online world of porn, and catfishing is on the rise. Innocent people are being taken advantage of by those looking to publicly shame them or extort money with photos that aren't of them. One of my girls had this happen to her. Then a couple years later, her name and likeness were stolen to set up a porn site that people had to pay to go see. They targeted all the men who follow her on social media. Shit is crazy out there, parents, so be aware. Put down your phones and pay attention to what's happening on your kid's devices.

♡ And, as always, I encourage you to go get your sexy on.

*Chapter Ten*

# ADULTING ON THEIR OWN

We've made it this far! I've opened your eyes to things that are happening in the world of high school/university-aged kids. Some of it you may have already known, but some of it may have come as a total surprise to you. There's a lot of stuff on social media that you might not be privy to if you, like me, are mostly on there looking at inspirational quotes, or at some celebs you think are hilarious, or at your own friends and family, which is why you have to make sure you ask your kid the tough questions, starting with "Hey, do you (or have you ever asked somebody to) share naked photos on social media?"

They may not answer you truthfully, which is why you need their passcodes. Having nudes of anybody under the age of consent is a felony, so you need to know if your kid is participating in this behavior since the consequences can be grave. So, be aware. Be involved. I cannot stress this enough. These are not the years to let them go it alone. These are the years to be more involved with them personally . . . asking questions all the time.

All my advice is why I'm your new best friend! I will tell you the whole truth and nothing but the truth, even if it gives you a heart attack, metaphorically speaking. But the great news is that I am also arming you with knowledge on how to combat these things so you're not blindsided after it's too late.

And that is a very good thing.

Right?

Right.


Okay, let's keep keeping on. We're almost at the end of the experiences I found myself in the thick of as a mom with no real knowledge of how to get my kids through them, and this next topic is super important for so many reasons, primarily because you love your kid, but you don't want them living under your roof forever. I mean, like, how are you going to go back to having sex on the couch or the kitchen counter if your kids are still around?

You won't.

You need to get your kid primed and ready to vacate the premises as soon as they're financially sound to do so, and the younger you start teaching them how to make money (and how to keep it!), the sooner they will move out. Now, I'm not suggesting you shove them out the door the second they graduate high school, but life is expensive out there, and is only getting more expensive, so one has to get on this particular adulting topic, like yesterday.

So often we think that hand-holding and doing all the things for them all the time is loving them more. I know that for me, since I grew up with a single mom and had a job since I was twelve, my tendency is to give, give, give and let it RAIN DOWN ON MY GIRLS! And I have to seriously fight that urge pretty hard, so I'm not judging you if you're a giver. I'm just saying that you must not give into everything, as it truly doesn't make for the strongest adults. Giving excessively actually has the opposite effect on them—it breeds a sense of entitlement and, dare I say, encourages laziness. When your kids know that Mommy and Daddy will always catch them when they fall, or clean up their messes, it's not very likely that they will grow a backbone strong enough to hold their own or become their own person. It's super important that we parents not give them the easy way out; it is imperative to parent them in a way that gives them the skills they need to land in shit, then pick themselves up, dust themselves off, and save their own skin.

When Yannick and I were expecting our first daughter, we thought Yannick's first regular TV gig was going to go on forever, so we rented an entire house and bought a couple of cars and all new furniture. But before we knew it, we were in our accountant's office, filing for bankruptcy. And nobody could help us. Neither of my parents had the means to rescue us, nor did either one of his. So, we learned, somewhat, how to be better with our money. (I say "somewhat" because two creatives in one household . . . well, you can guess that finances weren't a strength for either of us.) Over time, however, we learned to invest wisely in real estate and used our creative natures to flip houses, which helped us tremendously in becoming more financially sound. So, you see, when your kids have no net to catch them, they have no other choice but to figure out how to dig themselves out of the hole themselves! Letting them adult, educating them on the importance of budgeting, running, managing, and organizing a household, makes them better humans for themselves and dream partners for someone else should they decide to share their lives with somebody. I added this chapter to this teen book because I fully believe that my advice will up their chances of not becoming a divorce statistic! I remember reading many, many moons ago how financial strain was more of a precursor to divorce, ahead of infidelity. My marriage survived both, and I must say I have to agree that being literally broke was much harder to live through. But that's another story for another time.

## A FAIR WAGE FOR AN HONEST JOB WELL DONE

Hopefully, even if you didn't read my book on raising your littles, which I'm only a little bit offended by, you started your kids doing chores and getting paid for them already. I'm optimistic that assigning chores isn't new information to you . . .

Now, there are some children's therapists (and a lot of bloggers) who are anti-chore and payment. And then there are some people who think kids should do chores because it's simply about being a good member of the family unit—the whole "everybody does their part" mentality. And I totally agree. I totally see the logic and reasoning behind it, and we did a bit of both with our girls. When they were little, they got paid for their contributions to keeping the house. As they got older and had part-time jobs (which we'll go into a little bit later), we dialed back the allowances, and they helped around the house simply because they lived in it, they made it dirty, and, well, Yannick and I would make dinner, so they would clean up after it. It was called balance.

I think you can tell by now that I'm a big fan of balance in parenting and in my expectations of my girls. And I'd like to add that we tried to be fair parents as well. We tried to put ourselves in their shoes. For example, we had one girl who was a seriously competitive athlete in high school and who consistently kept her grades high enough to be on the honor roll. She was maxed out on time and insisting she have a part-time job would have been unwise of us and impossible for her. So, she did not have to have a job, but we also weren't handing her money for every little thing. She had to learn that money was gifted to her on special occasions, such as birthdays and Christmas, and if she wanted to make sure she had enough to go around during the school year, she had to budget. She had to watch her pennies, and she did. She learned quite quickly that if she shopped her heart out one week and then wanted to go to the movies with her friends the next, well, if there was no money left in her account, then there were no movies.

Our other two girls lost interest in their sports before they got to high school, so they had to have jobs. When kids are busy and not bored with too much time on their hands, it is less likely that they're going to get up to no good. So, it was win-win for our girls. When they were small, they earned their money, and it was theirs to spend how they wanted. If there was a big-ticket item they had their eye on, they had to save to get it. Our girls got gifts on their birthdays and Christmas. They got new clothes at the turn of the season if they'd grown out of stuff and if their sister's hand-me-downs no longer fit.

We taught them very early on that money doesn't grow on trees, that it needs to be earned, and that not every whim/want gets rewarded. I am all about the abundant mindset and everything, but it's important to respect money—the energy it takes to earn it and to stop with the instant gratification as a means to numb out or pacify a problem. We instilled in our daughters the value of how much time it takes to work to afford those new shoes or the trendy jacket everybody's wearing. It made them appreciate and respect the cost of acquiring new things. It also helped them sit back, reflect, and ponder whether they still really wanted that item after a month of babysitting or working customer service at Best Buy. It helped them become discerning about fulfilling every single WANT that crossed their mind and reduced their impulse to keep up with their peers' senseless, mindless consumerism.

I highly recommend you reserve gifts and toys for special occasions and new clothes for the change of seasons, and only if they've grown out of something. Make your kid save and buy the "extras" in their lives out of their own hard-earned money. It will be so useful to them as adults to have trained themselves to use caution and reason when it comes to buying shit. I mean, let's be honest here: The planet will thank you for raising conscientious, socially responsible consumers rather than zombie consumers who run out and buy, buy, buy!

## TEACH THEM ABOUT HAVING TO PAY THE TAX MAN

Listen, nobody likes to pay the tax man. There's not one person who sits down every month and says, "Wow! I gave almost half of the money I earned to my government. That's so cool!" Nope. I've never said it, and I'm sure you haven't either. But it is our reality. So, make sure they understand how taxing works.

Our girls are all in occupations where they're their own bosses. Two creatives gave birth to more creatives. Like, wow, what a surprise right?! Anyway, lucky for them, Yannick and I had already totally fucked up in our early years together and had a bankruptcy under our belts to remind us, and our kids, that the money you bring in will be taxed at some point. And that's where we got caught out. So, do your child(ren) a favor and let them know about the taxation system and the percentages based on earning. Teach them that they need to put this money aside in an account that they never touch. Period. End of story. And you may wish to seek advice from a financial consultant who understands how to make the money—that you and your kids have worked damn hard to earn!—work smarter for you.

Do your money homework so you can pass it down to your kid.

This way, they will, you know, move out.

## COMPOUNDING INTEREST

Oh, this is a juicy, ugly one! Credit card companies and banks love compounding interest! Banks thrive in giving university-aged kids credit cards. Each of our girls got one because credit cards "build their credit and teach them responsibility." Blah, blah, blah. The reality? It's an exercise in "How many Venti lattes and designer shoes will my kid purchase and pay 19.99 percent interest on for two years until we finally decide they've suffered enough so pay off their card just the one time?"

Yeah, you're likely to do the same for your kid at least once in their life. And FYI, we had our kids cut up their card after just such an outcome.

Teaching your kid how to use a credit card responsibly is a great way for them to learn about budgeting and restraint. Now, I'm not saying they're always going to listen to you, and that's okay. Growing up has to hurt sometimes. My motto is that if they won't listen, then they'll learn the hard way. But whether they learn the easy way or not, you will be raising an independent human being.

> Make your kid save and buy the "extras" in their lives out of their own hard-earned money.

## PAYING BILLS

I'm about to age myself again, but it has to be said: Young people freak me out. They do every single thing on their phones. Like E.V.E.R.Y.T.H.I.N.G. The only thing that got me banking on my iPhone was the damn pandemic because the banks either had long lines or bad hours. So, 2020 was the first time you saw this woman deposit her checks on her phone. And I didn't like it, not at all, especially after hearing that a friend of mine with a super successful business was hacked. The hackers took over all his bank accounts, and it took him MONTHS to get HIS accounts back! Jesus. What a nightmare!

But here we are . . . everybody's banking on their phones. But being victims of theft isn't the only concern I have for my daughters. What I've seen with my girls is that it's difficult for them to keep track of what's coming in and what's going out if they don't have it all written out in front of them, including the dates that bill payments are withdrawn. Now, I know you're probably thinking, "What bills does my fourteen-year-old have, Shantelle?"

Well, how about you give them one? Like have them pay half their phone bill each month. Or half of their public transit pass. Or a portion of their lunches at school.

It can be anything, really, that you ask them to pitch in on. And it doesn't even need to be because you need the cash. The idea is that you are teaching them the art of paying for what they have in their lives. It gives them a sense of appreciation when they have to pay for stuff, and they take better care of something if they know if it gets lost or broken, they're on their own to replace it.

You're creating a well-rounded individual here, people, somebody who will make a great employee and a wonderful partner to someone. A human who has value for all things, including how hard one has to work to have nice things. So, get them to balance their bank account—use whatever computer system you want. Get them having some financial responsibilities that they need to pay on time. Teach them how money works, and where it goes. Do this and prepare them for real life!

## SAVING FOR A RAINY DAY

And last but not least, teach your teen that just because they made $1,000 at their summer job doesn't mean they spend it all on the new iPhone. Teach them about taking at least 10 percent and putting it aside for a rainy day, as it were. Or, the fact that it is 2021, teach them to save 10 percent from the time they are born—that way, they just might be able to rent a bachelor apartment in the city one day!

Good Lord, what the hell is going on out there?! It's insanity, with no signs of slowing down. So, teach your kids the value of keeping a little bit from what they make off to the side so that one day, should they want to take that trip or buy that house, they will be able to. Now, chances are they're going to need to move some distance away from you if they hope to have a home of their own. And with jobs being scarce thanks to the pandemic, they may need to leave the country to get employment.

"Wow, Shantelle, you're so negative. I hate you! Say something upbeat, for God's sake!"

Listen, you read in the opening of this book that I was going to be blunt and speak nothing but the truth to you, and I am. I have three different scenarios with my kids. One lives in a condo in downtown Toronto with her husband—they rent because I'm not in a position to gift them a house in my neighborhood where they can raise their babies. They're currently looking to move into their own home, some two hours away. Not ideal, but it is what it is. Then we have our middle girl renting an apartment in Los Angeles, and our youngest, an actress who resides in our Toronto home with us.

It is tough out there, my friends. So, get them saving and preparing for life early. I can honestly say that Yannick and I didn't do it as well as we should have, so we tried to pass along to our girls to do the things we wish we'd done more diligently when it comes to money and how to manage and keep it, and now I'm hopefully passing it on to you.

## LET THEM PURSUE THEIR PASSIONS

One thing I do feel we did right when it came to money is that we scraped our artist money together to send our girls to the best schools in Toronto. Way, way back when our girls were little, Yannick and I read Dr. Mary Pipher's book *Reviving Ophelia*, as I mentioned earlier, and we was profoundly affected by her conviction that girls in grades seven and eight experience a single-sex education. We were struck by Dr. Pipher's explanation of the benefits of girls not being all wrapped up in male energy or the quest to win male approval during those hormonally imbalanced/charged years, so we went into debt to send them to an all-girls' school. Secretly, we also hoped that having our girls hobnobbing and hanging out with kids who had predilections to become doctors, lawyers, architects, and engineers would rub off on our artsy-fartsy girls.

Wanna guess how that turned out?

Well, I noted that they are all self-employed, and in creative occupations, so . . .

But I don't begrudge them. They still grew up with powerful voices, with strong opinions, and with the ability to hold their own in heated conversations on all topics, which is what Dr. Pipher said would happen if we could at least give them those two years in a single-sex education system. Now, would they have been that way anyway? I don't know, but I can say that they all stood their own in their university lecture halls, and they continue to do so in situations with strong domineering male energy to this day. So, what does any of this have to do with making sure they follow their passions?

I'm going to tell you right now.

Because life is simultaneously too short and too long to spend it not living your passion.

And that's the tea.

That's it.

Need I say more?

Okay, if you insist. I'll say this:

You can't take it with you when you go. I've never seen a U-Haul behind a hearse.

So, really, how well is a life lived if we raise our children to chase cash instead of dreams? How content are they going to be if they spend their lives buried in work? I encourage you to be the parent who supports them in their quest to live a life that feels good to them so they are happy—deeply, profoundly happy— in their own skin. I support you in doing the work to release your expectations of what you would like your kid to become, or where you would like them to live, or who you would like them to marry. It isn't your life, it's your kid's. Let them color it in a way that feels best to them. And like I've always said to my girls, "As long as how you live isn't hurting anybody else, then I'm good if you're good."

Take it from a woman who didn't end up with a single doctor—it is just as rewarding to see your children living passionately as it is to see them wealthy! And who knows? Perhaps the wealth will come, since they're living wholly and truthfully!

*Things to Nibble On*

♡ Get your kids to help around the house, and the sooner the better. Pay them so they understand the value of earning money.

♡ Teach them about their duty to pay taxes. Put a positive spin on it. Explain about public services/schools or anything else you want to sprinkle on there to make paying those steep taxes easier to swallow.

♡ Please, for the love of God, teach them about interest on debt. Not that they're going to listen to you. I mean, it seems every kid needs to learn about interest rates the hard way, but at least your conscience will be clear when they come crying to you about how they still haven't paid for those Dior sunglasses they bought two years ago!

♡ Teach them about bills, due dates, and balancing their checkbooks. They'll need to know how when monthly expenses start to roll in.

♡ We never know what life is going to throw at us, so make sure you encourage your children to save for their future and to put some money aside in case, you know, we face a global pandemic or something.

♡ Encourage them to find an occupation or career that they're passionate about, even if it's not what you would have wanted for them. Remind yourself that it is their life to live, not yours. Let them have the freedom to live true to their dreams.

# Chapter Eleven

# MOMMY MADNESS

As I'm sure you've noticed by now, I am not a perfect mother, and if you read my first book, *Raising Your Kids Without Losing Your Cool*, you already knew that about me. I'm known for saying, "Perfection has no place in parenting," and it doesn't. Ever. Not once should you aspire to be a perfect parent. Is it a good idea to aim to be the BEST parent you can be? Yes, always, every day. Even on your off/bad days, you must strive to be your best worst version of yourself. But perfection? Nah. That shit is something we leave for show dogs and racehorses. Not human beings. And certainly not parents.

I mean, how does one even begin to achieve perfection in parenting? If somebody has that on lock, I'd like them to reach out to me and give me their secrets. I was so far from perfect as a parent that some may have called me unfit a time or two. And by "some," I mean my three daughters. You see, I didn't write this book for you because I was such a shining example of a patient, kind, loving, and level-headed mom every single day of my teen parenting years that of course my daughters turned out to be awesome adults. Please take note of how I said they turned out to be *awesome*, not *perfect*. I didn't say that my girls grew into perfect adults because there is no such thing as perfection in being human, whether a child or parent. So, the sooner you let go of the illusion that somebody out there on social media, or even closer to home than that is perfect, the sooner you will be happier in your own parent/kid relationships. Trust me on this one—trying to wear the skin of a "perfect" parent you don't actually have any cold, hard facts on will only drive you mad.

Keep your eyes on your own garden.

Once, back in the '90s, a mom from the church I belonged to felt the need to share with me some things she had observed "in passing" about one of my daughters. Well, I found her note hilarious, not because her observations about my daughter weren't accurate (they were) but because I had witnessed firsthand on *many* occasions two of her daughters suffering from severe drug and alcohol hangovers. This woman was so busy looking around and finding fault in others that she was completely oblivious to what was happening right under her nose. My mind was completely blown. It was my first run-in with what I like to call delusional-parenting syndrome.

I don't recommend having this sort of arrogance. It's better to err on the side of "I'm a complete mess" than it is to believe you're a perfect parent with perfect children. So be cool. Keep your eyes on your own garden, and let other parents manage theirs. You'll probably end up with way more friends in your parent circle if you keep your opinions of other people's kids to yourself. It's not our jobs to educate people on their kids' shortcomings or character flaws. And if someone asks you for insight into their kid, TREAD LIGHTLY. I've made this mistake, my friend, and it's a deep, deep hole to dig back out of. The best way to be a good friend to someone who is struggling with their teen's behavior is to *not* talk about their kid specifically but to use examples of how you would deal with it if it were your kid or cite articles you may have read that tackle that issue. And if you're at a loss as to how to help a fellow parent in the thick of teendom? Direct them to me. Have them buy my book! That totally takes all the heat off you. Problem solved.

I have a number of friends with children, some older, the same age as, or younger than my three girls, and when I ask them about how easy their parenting journeys have been, they're always blunt: It's tough as shit. We've all experienced many, *many* days of parenting that have been downright terrifying. Like when our teens first got their driver's licenses, for example. I can't tell you how many nights I was wide awake in bed certain that my baby was wrapped around a pole somewhere. Yes, I'm a dramatic person (who was truly destined for the stage until, you know, I wasn't), but my point is valid. You will feel like you're losing your fucking mind so often that you'll probably start drinking, if you haven't already. (Another thing I was famous for saying was, "I'm not an alcoholic, I'm just the mother of teenage girls.")

There are going to be so many unknowns that come your way, and there's no way for me to begin to predict what things your child will get involved in that will scare the hell out of you. If you're fortunate, like we were with our third, you will have a teen who doesn't break a single rule. Not one. You'll never have to nag them to respect their curfew, as they're always home . . . early. You'll not once need to ask them about homework assignments, as they're already completed . . . also early. You may never experience raised voices or harsh words. I know those kinds of kids are out there because we had one. But, and not to upset your applecart here, if you have a teenager like that, they may end up with some emotional issues because they are too worried about fucking up and letting you down to live life like a human being.

Basically, what I'm saying here is that you can't predict how your kid(s) will go through their teen years any more than you can predict the weather. But the point of this chapter is to let you know that nobody, parent and child alike, gets through the teen years unscathed, and there is no parent out there who is going to navigate these years perfectly. I have so many mom-fail stories that honestly, they could fill their own book. I've said things I can never take back in the heat of the moment. I've lashed out both verbally and physically, and if I could dial back the hands of time, I would go back as the woman I am today, with the tools I now have for conflict resolution and the training I've acquired over the years for defusing heated situations, and I'd do it so differently. I wouldn't make any of those old mistakes.

Now, chances are I would make new ones, because isn't that how life works? Just when you master one part of yourself on this journey called life, something else pops up that challenges you in every way, which is in and of itself the entire parenting paradox.

But I cannot go back. So, I wrote this book. For you. To help you avoid some of these moments in your own parenting journey. It is full of the things that I did right when I was my best, most level-headed and calm self. Those things, those solid core values, were the poured concrete of raising my girls—the foundation of their humanness that carried them through my worst moments. All the great momming I did was more than enough to get us back on track in our relationships. Apologies were given and received. Vows were made and upheld. Changes were made and deeper more respectful bonds were created. And this, my friends, is the key to creating a deep, loving, and mutually beneficial relationship with your teen: admitting when you've fucked up. Owning it. Apologizing for it without any *ifs* or *buts*. You know what they are. "I'm so sorry I hit you, but Mommy freaked out because you called me a bitch."

You see the *but* in that apology.

And yes, a similar situation will likely happen to you, and when it does, hitting them isn't the answer. It may be your natural reflex and urge to hit them because, I mean, you've lost years of sleep, you've spent hours driving them all over God's green earth, you've been name-called and ignored—all the reasons you'll be set off, but not one of them is good enough to make them think that your negative reaction happened because of their behavior. Believe me when I say it takes the control of a saint to be the adult and remind yourself (which I didn't do enough of) that it's not about you, it's them. You may need to take seventy-five deep breaths or go lock yourself in your room and punch your pillow; I don't know what you'll need to do to not react the way I did, but I encourage you to figure out what works for you.

I want you to know that even if you feel like some days/weeks/months are just fail after fail after fail that I, too, felt completely lost more times than I would have liked when I was parenting my teens. I was overwhelmed. Insecure. Unsure that I was raising them in a balanced way. Was I too lenient on some issues (like letting them drink alcohol with us) and then too strict on other things (like not letting them go away on trips alone with friends)? I don't know. I did

> Be consistent.
> Consistent in love.
> Consistent in support.
> Consistent with your
> boundaries. Consistent
> with hope—hope that it
> will all turn out okay.

what I felt was the best for them at the time. If you're a parent who has it on their heart to do their absolute best with raising their teen

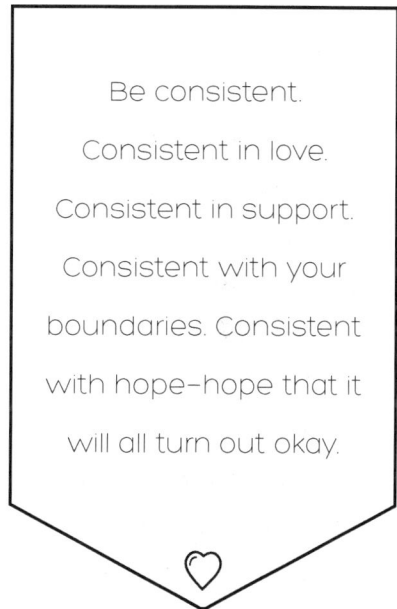

into an awesome, well-rounded adult, don't keep yourself up at night second-guessing if you're doing it "right." Relax, stop stressing out about all the crazy thoughts and doubts you might be having, and trust that your teen knows you love them and that you're in their corner. And if it feels like right now you are miles apart from your teen and they won't let you in, be consistent. Consistent in love. Consistent in support. Consistent with your boundaries. Consistent with hope—hope that it will all turn out okay.

And if there are areas in your relationship with your teen that you feel out of your depth in, call in experts, get help, and get support—get an extra helping hand to get you to the other side. I'm a mom who is far on the other side of the teen years, yet I can still take myself back there in less than a second flat! I have to tell you that even in the thick of it all, in the times I overreacted to broken curfews, lies, and name-calling, there were also glorious moments of complete and utter bliss and joy in raising my three girls during their teen years. And the victories are as easy to recall as the bad moments. We had movie marathons in our pjs in my bed, sang carpool karaoke, and had kitchen dance parties. Every element of my mom journey plays back like a favorite movie with all the key elements: drama, suspense, and love. Lots and lots of love. And you will have these moments too. The glory of a hard-fought battle won. The tremendous sense of accomplishment that one gets when they get a kid to high school graduation is not to be taken lightly and certainly nothing to be scoffed at. You and I both know that the teen years are scary. Your beautiful, easygoing child will flip-flop from hot to cold to hot, and often. But they will also blossom into their own human being, one with convictions, strengths, dreams, and ambitions, and you will find yourself cheering them on from the sidelines. But know that to get there, to get to that massive moment in time, you must go through all the other stuff—some magical and some horrible. Just keep in mind that whether it's magical or horrible, nothing lasts forever.

This too shall pass. And it does.

I'm hoping that what you've gleaned from my parenting experiences is just how many different potential scenarios you might find yourself in during life with a teen. Some things are maybes: You may not have a child who grapples with their gender identity and how they can tell you and the world who they really are inside. Other things I can guarantee: If you have a child on social media, they will be contacted by a predator in some way. No matter what you end up facing as the parent of a teen, it is my wish that at least now you know you are not alone. I fucked up so royally and so regularly in my parenting and yet ended up with beautiful, healthy, close relationships with all three of my girls, so you, who will definitely do better than I did, will be okay. And if you don't do better than I did, because so much about being a parent is trial and error, it will still all be okay in the end as long as you lead with love. If you find yourself totally and completely losing your cool, time and time again, remember that if you apologize from your heart with true humility and sincerity, and you've raised decent people who understand that we all are just human and we all mess up, then they will forgive you. They will forgive you in the same way you, as their parent, forgive them when they're little assholes. And herein lies the secret of regaining your cool after you've lost it: Forgive yourself and let go!

*Final Nibbles*

Before I let you leave this book behind, I want to recap the guts of it for you right here. Consider it a cheat sheet for getting through the teen years without losing your cool or, at the very least, going gray. The bottom line is this: Your intention is to raise a strong, independent human being who can weather any storm. If life goes as one hopes it will, our children will outlive us, meaning we won't always be there for them. And I know every parent wants their teen to grow into the sort of person who solves life issues on their own. We parents are all striving to achieve independence—them from us, and us from them. And this is how we get it done:

**1) Your teen isn't out to get you!** They're working through so much shit: hormones, hierarchies at school and, for some kids, gender and sexuality issues. BE COOL. Don't take everything that comes out of their mouth as a personal attack. Let some of it roll off your back, like a duck in water. Be like that duck. But while you let them work out their shit, remind them that they still need to do so respectfully under your roof. Teach them to move through their growing pains with grace and respect. You won't do them any favors in this giant world of ours if you let them be belligerent assholes. You need to prepare your teen for *real life*, not life in the cozy bubble of your home where they are treated like the most awesome, wonderful, brilliant human to walk the earth. Now, I'm not telling you that you shouldn't be your kid's biggest fan *or* that you should hang them out to dry, leaving them on their own to "sort it all out." Not at all. I'm reminding you that you need to parent/ guide/teach them with balance. Be tough on them when they need you to be tough on them. Tell them *no*. Make sure you have nonnegotiable rules in place that are there for their safety. Teach them in order to get ahead, they have to do it with character, intellect, and knowledge, not with brute force or bullying. Teach them that hard work equals reward. The world won't come to them on a silver platter, so don't send them out into the world believing that it will.

**2) Be humble.** Practice humility. Admit when you fuck up. You're human. You're probably going to do it a lot, so *own* it. By owning your bullshit and your meltdowns or overreactions, you'll show your teen how to deal with people outside your family when they melt down or blow up. It also teaches them something even more valuable—a mindset that is sadly dying out in our modern society: It's not a sign of weakness to apologize when you're wrong. Life isn't about being right or winning an argument. You're teaching them that it is, in fact, the complete opposite. Life is better lived if it's done with love and humility. It takes great strength to look somebody dead in the eye and say the words *I am sorry*. In doing so, you teach your teen about letting go, about forgiveness, and about how absolutely amazing it feels to be apologized to. Teens can smell bullshit a mile away and don't appreciate being treated like babies. So, be honest with them, be frank with them, and be humble. They respond to humility, and often, if your kids are like mine, they will accept your apology wholeheartedly, tell you that they love you, then walk away from the situation thinking that you're pretty fucking cool! And when they go out into the world and have relationships with all kinds of people, they will show others how powerful an apology can be.

**3) Now that you have teens under your roof,** you're getting super close to that moment in time when your kids will grow up and leave, so contrary to popular belief, they are not your most important relationship in your family. Make sure that you never stop working on bettering yourself, feeding your soul, and taking amazing care of *you*. And if you have a partner, your next most important relationship is the one you have with them. Too many people have teens with demanding schedules—competitive sports, tutoring, art classes, a million things that require that they drive them all over—and so they let their partner hang out on the back burner of their lives while the kids become their focus. Don't let this happen. Make your significant other the one you nurture, love, and care for first. Set the bar high. You want your teens to see what a healthy, loving, important relationship looks like so that they imitate it in their own young romances. They will be able to thrive in a strong, happy relationship and will bring up confident, secure young adults of their own. And that is exactly the sort of cycle we want to create. Plus, by being deeply connected, you will create a solid parenting team. You will have more support in your decisions, and therefore, you will have more energy for other things, like *sex*. Which, if you haven't figured out by now, you should be doing a lot!

*Chapter Twelve*

# YOU SURVIVED TEENDOM. NOW WHAT?

Alright, we did it! We made it through this book that breaks down the trials, tribulations, and potential teen scenarios you'll probably find yourself facing with your kid. Perhaps you've read the book front to back and you've already encountered one situation, if not more. Perhaps you haven't had to deal with any of them yet or, if you're really lucky, you're on the other side of teendom and never did. And if that's you, whether you recognize yourself and your teen(s) in these pages, I want to say one thing: You did it. You're here, on the other side of being in the dark. You kept your cool. You got them to the age of what I like to call Stage I of cutting the cord. They're through high school, with their next steps in life plotted out, whether it be a gap year, or two, or three, or many (like me). Or maybe they're heading immediately to college or university. Wherever they go, you can be confident with the knowledge that they're taking a massive piece of you with them. And no, I don't mean your heart (though they definitely take that with them). They take with them your teachings, your guidance, your wisdom,

> You got through it together with the love, unity, and strength of the parent-child bond.

and your love.

I know where you've been hasn't been easy. I know there were times you probably curled up in a ball and sobbed out of worry—out of concern for their safety. You were anxious about their future. You were troubled over a partner you knew wasn't good for them, somebody who undid the best parts of them, and you wondered if your kid would ever snap out of it and crawl out from under their spell. You watched them have a brush with drugs and alcohol and worried it would become an addiction. You held them while they cried over being ostracized and bullied to the point you were concerned they might break. But they didn't, and you didn't. You got through it together with the love, unity, and strength of the parent-child bond, and now you are here in this next stage of your parenting journey, and you're once again headed into uncharted territory. You will have new roads to cross and new challenges to help parent them through. That is, after all, the lifelong journey of the role of parent. We are constantly teaching, forever guiding, and always loving.

But there is cause for celebration. Because before you read this book, before you conquered all the unknowns that were coming your way, you were unsure and a bit nervous about how the teen years were going to go for you. What would you do if your child developed an eating disorder? What if your child doesn't identify with the gender they were assigned at birth? There are so many pieces of being a parent that you don't think about while your child is tiny and you're (barely) functioning on only a few sporadic hours of sleep here and there. Those days were rough, yet you survived!

Then you got here, to this place of getting to know the alien in your house, and you fell in love all over again as they developed and stood up for who they are in their souls. And as they expressed their individuality and forged their identities, your love for them grew deeper. Your bond and understanding of who they are as human beings, and not simply your child, blossomed. The ever-evolving exploration of being a parent is a beautiful journey. The more you release your own expectations of what being a parent means for you, and the more you dive into being the parent your child needs you to be, the more peaceful the relationship will be.

Listen. Ask questions. Trust. Respect. Your bond will become tighter as a result.

I vividly remember thinking at one point that my mother was a pushover. I was dating somebody she didn't like, and when my mother gave me her advice, for probably the six millionth time, I ignored it, and she did nothing. She didn't fight with me. She didn't ground me. She didn't threaten me or say that I would come to regret it. She simply let me be. She let me live out the experience. I thought I had "won" and that she mustn't really care if she wasn't going to force me to do what she thought was the right thing. So, years later when I found myself at similar crossroads with my own daughters, I did as my mother did: I gave my two cents, shared how I would move forward if in the same situation, then let them make their own choices. Why? Well, it is a powerful teaching opportunity to let them move through life making their own decisions and consequently, their own mistakes. Additionally, it showed them that I trusted them to do what felt right for them. Plus, it finally gave me the opportunity to show them that when they didn't do as I said and the shit hit the fan for them, that no matter whether we agreed or not, I would always be there to catch them if/when they fell.

And that is key. No matter what your kid does, they need to know that you will always be there on the other side to catch them, to love them, to forgive them. They need to know that they are safe and that there is no judgment or shame in failing, only learning. Now obviously, and I think you know this already, I'm not saying that you let your kid run wild, harming themselves and those around them. You know I mean that you let your kid learn to fall and blow it as long as they're safe. If they're behaving in ways that puts their own safety or the safety of others around them in jeopardy, then you always, always step in. And you need to be even more on top of it once they go away to school. Being away at school . . . oh, man, that's a whole other load of shit for sleepless nights, for real.

But let's not go there. You only just arrived here at this place, which is way more informed than you were just a few hours ago! You have now decided that there is much more power in healing and letting go of any hurt or unresolved negative emotions you may have been holding on to with your ex. You know that your kids are much better off living between two homes that are unified and at peace with one another. You have gained knowledge about eating disorders and self-harm and know what signs to watch out for. You understand that how/when your teen behaves like a total asshole has everything to do with them and not you (unless you, too, are an asshole). You're empowered because you know that you're not alone, that others have gone before you and survived, and that you should get outside help if you need it. And to that I say, YAY, YOU! I'm proud of you. Parenting is not for the faint of heart, nor is it for quitters, and I commend you for your commitment to doing the most to do your best. So many get to this stage, this wild and crazy stage of what-the-fuck-happened-to-my-child, and they want to check out. It is so much easier to leave them to their own devices, whether that means allowing them to run with the wrong crowd of kids, or abuse alcohol or drugs, or be sexually promiscuous. It is so much simpler in the moment to just let it all slide—because honestly, who wants to fight every single day of their lives with a person who has no barometer with which to govern themselves?

I will never forget all the things I put my mother through. The bullshit I said and the asshole ways I behaved, over and over again. I remember thinking, in all my worldly wisdom of like fourteen, that my mom was old and uncool. Super uncool. I can clearly recall thinking she was jealous of my youth and the fact that the "cool" kids wanted me to hang out with them. There was a group of older kids at my high school known as "The Muscle Beach Gang," and yes,

> It is a powerful teaching opportunity to let them move through life making their own decisions and consequently, their own mistakes.

it is exactly as you would suspect it would be—a group of guys who ate copious amounts of animal protein, drove hot rods, and worked out. I do believe a few of them were also using steroids, as they certainly had some of the telltale signs: engorged nipples and backne (acne on their backs). But this little rant isn't about them, entirely, it's more about me. This gang of guys wanted to add me, a minor-niner, to their crew, and my mother was not at all cool with it. Like not in the slightest. And now, looking back as a mother of daughters who all went through the teen years, and knowing so much more about the male mind than I did back then, I can totally see why my mom was like, "Ahhhh, hell no."

Did I listen to my mother?

What do you think?

Of course, I didn't. I hung out with them anyway. And I hung out with them until one of them tried to convince me that I should give him my "virginity." (I put this word in parenthesis because mine was already stolen at age twelve, so it wasn't actually for him to have, but he wanted to be the first to have consensual sex with me.) Lucky for me, he was a decent guy and didn't force the issue or my decision when I said no to him. But what this experience did teach me was that my mother was right. My mother was smart. My mother loved me and was trying to protect me. Did I ease up on being a pain in her ass?

Of course, I didn't.

But I did stop hanging out with that crew of guys, pronto.

Why this trip down memory lane? Because the moral of this story is that your children may not appear to be listening to you when you lay down rules, give them guidelines, or advise them on what you feel they should or should not do or with whom they should or should not associate. They will try this stuff on for size, and when they realize that you were right, they will make the best choice for themselves—the safe, smart, and correct choice for their higher self.

You can totally trust me on this one.

And you know you can because I was pretty much the worst kid you could imagine. I didn't trust, or listen, or respect, but I grew into a person who did, and I, in turn, managed to raise three women who also went sideways during their struggles through adolescence and teendom and came out okay. They grew into women who respect other people's boundaries and have curious minds that question the world around them without being disrespectful to others with varying opinions.

And that, my friends, is the key.

Being consistent, firm, and loving with your children, while giving them boundaries balanced with freedom, creates people who can adult in a world with confidence and respect toward others. You deciding to never give up or throw in the towel, even after you've had the same argument with them for the hundred-thousandth time, gets you a beautiful, important, healthy, strong relationship with a human being that is your favorite person—somebody you'd hang out with before all others should they call you and say they want to go for lunch or to a movie.

You did this.

You made them.

Well done, you! So, now that we're at the end of our journey together, let me take this moment to remind you that parenting is **A MARA-THON, NOT A SPRINT.**

I'm confident that many things have gone exactly as you planned and many others didn't, which is how life goes. I'm confident you did an awesome job of circling the wagons during the storms. You sought support, advice, and guidance from professional people when the need for them was necessary, or you leaned on others you know and love who faced similar parenting challenges and came out the other side. All in all, you didn't try to go it alone, living in the fear of the situation you found yourself in. You removed ego and parented from love. I see you. I respect you. I've been you, so I know it hasn't been a walk in the park, and I want you to know that regardless of what the little voice inside your head is saying, you're doing great, and I am giving you a virtual high five.

If you've followed my advice, your child is a grounded kid who knows, without a doubt, that you love them. You've given them the tools they need to go out into the world on their own. You've made it this far, and now you'll be nodding your head in agreement when I list some character traits you recognize in your young human:

- a strong sense of self
- a tremendous amount of self-confidence
- an empathetic nature
- the ability to take the bull by the horns at school, in their extracurricular activities, and in their relationship with you, their peers, and their teachers. You probably have a little bit of an amateur debater—we had two of these, which is a very good thing.

You'll have peace of mind when they go out in the world because you'll know they can handle themselves, stand their ground, and meet conflict head on! You have a child who feels confident and trusting enough in their relationship with you to know that they can challenge your point of view on things without being told to "shut up and go to your room."

If you've practiced balance in your parenting, then you enter these young adult years knowing that no matter what storms come your way, you have the solid foundation of love and respect to weather them all. You trust them and they trust you. You respect them and they respect you, and as long as that is the cornerstone of your relationship with one another, you can't and won't go wrong.

But you must not let up. You must not go soft now. You cannot retreat, thinking your biggest battles are behind you. Don't get lazy or complacent because you think the journey is over. You *always* have to pay attention; you have to constantly be ready to ask the tough questions. Your consistent parenting will ensure that your kid always feels safe.

After all, they may not be a baby anymore, but they're still your "baby."
Now, onward and upward, rock-star parents!

xo *Shantelle*

P.S. Remember to keep having sex! Be intimate and make time for a soul connection with your partner. Taking care of those natural sexual urges is a great way to release stress, so make sure you *get it done!*

"There's always going to be someone faster, smarter, taller, more experienced than you, but the rewards in life don't always go to them; the rewards in life go to the dogged, the determined, those who can keep going and pick themselves back up and never say die and just hang in there, sometimes quietly and undramatically."[15]

Share this advice from Bear Grylls with your children; it can save their lives. Like, literally.

# ACKNOWLEDGMENTS

Obviously, the very first person who I owe a debt of gratitude to for being where I am in my life is my mother. Thank you for not killing me, Mom. Lord knows I gave you plenty of good reasons to do so with how I behaved, over and over and over again. Thank you for actually being so cool—dance parties in the car while driving around, making my costumes, taking me to my audition at Canada's Wonderland, and not losing your cool on me when your car was towed from getting stuck in somebody's driveway. You are a solid example of how to be an excellent mom. I'm so thankful it was you, and I'm even more thankful that you had the strength of character to not give up on me. I love you!

Brianna, Dominique, and Mikaela, what can I even say? You are my greatest accomplishments. You've taught me more about myself, this life, and who I want to be in this world by being my daughters. Writing this book took me straight back to all our shared experiences through your teen journeys. Some made me laugh out loud, some made me cry, and others gave me such a sense of joy and happiness, thanks to all the amazing experiences we've shared and all the memories we've made. Some of my personal favorites are traveling and seeing the world together. I'm beyond thankful to each of you for all that we've accomplished together. I'm definitely a way better human for having the gift of being a mom to the three of you. Thank you for being patient with me. Thanks for being my favorite people on the planet. Thank you for trusting me and for educating me in all the ways you did and continue to do. I love you so much, it actually hurts!

Yannick. There's not much else to share here that I haven't shared before all over social media, in my blogs, or in my other thank-yous. All I can say is that every day I wake up is my favorite day because I get to live it knowing that I have you in my corner as my lover, my partner, my friend, and my adventure buddy. It is a blessed situation we find ourselves in, having a love so deep and true, and I for one am not mad about it. Thanks for supporting me in all my ambitions and endeavors. I love you madly, my sexy man.

Jenanne, thank you for being the sister I never had and for being the best aunt to my three girls that I could have ever hoped for. They love you as much as I do (if not more!), and it fills my heart with so much happiness knowing that they always have you to turn to, no matter what. I could never have survived my teen years without you. You were by far the best thing that came out of them; well, I guess that was until "you know who" showed up! (He'll throw a fit if I don't put that in here!) Thanks for putting up with me through all the shit . . . and there was plenty of it! You're a keeper, and I love you.

Oh, Cheyanne, thanks for coming into our lives and starting a family as young as I did! I'm so grateful that you've always been by my side through all the good, the bad, and the ugly. You were sandwiched in between two Craigs, and somehow you haven't been crushed by the weight of that. I'm lucky to call you sister, and I'm grateful I had your shoulder to lean and cry on when parenting my girls through the teen years got super sketchy. You're top of my list of favorite people. I love you and am deeply grateful to have you in my corner.

Barbie . . . we've weathered so many similar storms, and your friendship and sisterhood has always meant the world to me. You've championed and guided me through so many messy, dark, scary moments, and I will never forget your love, your strength, your wisdom, and all our kitchen karaoke dance parties. Our shared laughter carried me through so many tough times. I'm blessed to still have you as the sister I chose after all these years. I love you and thank you!

Laura, seriously, even though you're a young mom and Luke is not even double digits, you were and continue to be one of the best things that ever happened to my girls during their formative years. I'm so fortunate that the universe brought you into our lives when it did . . . I had no idea what a rock you would be in my life and theirs. Thanks for always being consistent and for being a genuine and positive role model for my girls. I love you, lady!

Helen Heller, I know we still haven't managed to do a book with one another, but your faith in my ability to be a writer has never left me. Whenever I started to wonder whether I was a writer, I would hear your positive words in my head, and they would give me the confidence to write on. One of these days I'll finish those fiction books, and you'll be able to add me to your deep roster of best-selling fiction authors. Thanks for being an honest, generous friend. I'm truly thankful for all you've done for me over the years!

To YGTMedia Co. and Sabrina, I love what you're doing for aspiring authors. You've demystified the process while supporting us on our journey of sharing our stories and getting our messages out to those who need/want to hear them. Your never-ending support and authentic excitement in bringing these stories to light is so beautiful. You're a breath of fresh air in an otherwise claustrophobic industry. I'm so, so, so appreciative that you not only saw the value in carrying on my *Without Losing Your Cool* book series but that you believed that this teen book was a deeply important one that needed to be shared with parents everywhere. I'll never forget how you went above and beyond to help me round out my brand in order to allow this book to really shine and stand out in the crowded space of the parenting realm. I look forward to seeing what the future has in store for not only my career, but yours as well. Thanks for taking a chance on me! Thank you also for your incredible, brilliant crackerjack team who got this baby on the shelves in record time . . . I will never forget their commitment to my ridiculous timeline.

Speaking of your team: Tania, thank you for taking my ramblings and constructing them into a book that makes sense for the reader. I love what you've done with her, and thank you for cutting through all the extras to leave not only me but the reader with the straight goods!

Christine, I'm so grateful for your ability and gift to craft my words, my convictions, and my sloppy research into charts and bullet points that make sense and are, well, accurate pieces of knowledge. I'm so happy to have had your expertise and brilliance get her to the place where she actually reads like a book! Thank you, thank you, thank you!

And Doris . . . seriously! She's so beautiful. Thank you from the bottom of my heart for creating a book that looks great sitting on my shelf and looks just as pretty on the inside. You have a gift, lady, and I for one am grateful for it!

Leisse, you're a gift to me for SO MANY REASONS. All I want to do is make sure that my gratitude for all the gifts you have given me over the past year are written in ink for everyone to read for all of time. Thank you for introducing me to your publisher and for being one of those women who is actually a woman who helps lift other women up and helps them get where their souls aspire to be! Thank you for helping me heal the parts of me that were holding me back and that needed to be acknowledged, honored, and released. I will forever be grateful for the universe bringing you into my life. I know we'll be friends for the rest of our days, and I'm here for it!

And, of course, Nina. You're a Queen. Your resilience, brilliance, and light are gifts to me. I'm blown away by your support, your guidance, your humor, and, of course, your wisdom. My only hope is that you feel as supported, respected, and backed by me as I do you! Thank you for all you do every day to help me keep my eye on the prize.

Mr. Hall, my grade-nine English teacher, wherever you are, I hope you know that your confidence in me, along with your joy of teaching English, is alive and well in me. Your encouragement of my writing way back when has brought me here, and I hope that somehow you know that you did this for me, and I thank you from the bottom of my writer's heart!

And, of course, to all of you for buying this book and for inviting me into your lives and trusting me to help you raise warriors and lions who are capable of absolutely anything. I think I'm grateful for you the most!

xx Shantelle

# END NOTES

1. Elizabeth Stone quote. https://www.goodreads.com/quotes/14913-making-the-decision-to-have-a-child---it-is, retrieved April 28, 2021.

2. Elia Abi-Jaoude, Karline Treurnicht Naylor and Antonio Pignatiello. "Smart Phones, Social Media Use and Youth Mental Health." CMAJ. February 10, 2020. https://www.cmaj.ca/content/192/6/E136, retrieved May 9, 2021.

3. CDC. "Sexual Violence is Preventable." https://www.cdc.gov/injury/features/sexual-violence/index.html, retrieved April 28, 2021.

4. Chatterjee, Rhitu. "Daily Marijuana Use and High Potency Weed Linked to Psychosis." CapRadio. March 19, 2019. https://www.capradio.org/news/npr/story?storyid=704948217&, retrieved April 28, 2021.

5. CDC. "Sexual Violence is Preventable." https://www.cdc.gov/injury/features/sexual-violence/index.html, retrieved April 28, 2021.

6. High Focus Centers. "Early Warning Signs of Mental Illness in Teens." https://highfocuscenters.pyramidhealthcarepa.com/early-warning-signs-of-mental-illness-in-teens, retrieved April 28, 2021.

7. NEDA. "What Are Eating Disorders?" https://www.nationaleatingdisorders.org/what-are-eating-disorders, retrieved on April 28, 2021.

8. Mond, J. M., Mitchison, D., & Hay, P. Prevalence and implications of eating disordered behavior in men. In L. Cohn & R. Lemberg (Eds). *Current Findings on Males with Eating Disorders* (pp. 195-215). Routledge. 2014.

9. NEDA. "Warning Signs and Symptoms." https://www.nationaleatingdisorders.org/warning-signs-and-symptoms, retrieved May 9, 2021.

10. APA. "Who Self-Injures?" July/August 2015, Vol 46, No. 7. https://www.apa.org/monitor/2015/07-08/who-self-injures, retrieved April 28, 2021.

11. https://www.hopkinsmedicine.org/center-transgender-health/patient-resources/books.html

12. Graph 1: https://www.narcity.com/sugar-baby-universities-here-are-the-top-10-in-canada-for-2021, retrieved on April 28, 2021.

13. Graph 2: https://www.seeking.com/p/sugar-baby-university-2021/usa/, retrieved April 28, 2021.

14. Graph 3: https://www.seeking.com/p/sugar-baby-university-2021/usa/, retrieved April 28, 2021.

15. Bear Grylls in *If I Could Tell You Just One Thing: Encounters with Remarkable People and Their Most Valuable Advice* by Richard Reed. Chronicle Books, 2018.

# FURTHER READING

♡ *Real Talk About Sex and Consent: What Every Teen Needs to Know* by Cheryl M. Bradshaw

♡ *The Transgender Teen: A Handbook for Parents and Professionals Supporting Transgender and Non-Binary Teens* by Stephanie A. Brill and Lisa Kinney

♡ *Quiet: The Power of Introverts in a World That Can't Stop Talking* by Susan Cain

♡ *Protecting the Gift: Keeping Children and Teenagers Safe (and Parents Sane)* by Gavin de Becker

♡ *Drink: The Intimate Relationship Between Women and Alcohol* by Ann Dowsett Johnston

♡ *In Praise of Slowness: Challenging the Cult of Speed* by Carl Honore

♡ *Hunger Pains: The Modern Woman's Tragic Quest for Thinness* by Dr. Mary Pipher

♡ *Reviving Ophelia: Saving the Selves of Adolescent Girls* by Dr. Mary Pipher

♡ *If I Could Tell You One Thing* by Richard Reed

♡ *Me and My White Supremacy: Combat Racism, Change the World, and Become a Good Ancestor* by Layla F. Saad

# SHANTELLE BISSON

Two-time author Shantelle Bisson divides her time between Toronto, Los Angeles, and her marina, Shantilly's Place, in the Kawartha region of Ontario. In addition to being an author, producer, and recovering actress, Shantelle is mother to three beautiful daughters and two four-legged sons and is wife to Yannick Bisson, star of Canada's number one drama series, CBC's *Murdoch Mysteries*.

Shantelle believes strongly in giving back to the community. She sits on the committee of

Childhood Cancer Canada and has cochaired their main fundraising event, The Purple Party, since 2012. Her involvement has helped raise more than $1.5 million to date. Shantelle also supports Bridgepoint Active Healthcare via their annual fundraiser, The Heist, as a donor. Additionally, Shantelle and her husband give generously to the APJ fund, supporting kids in Haiti by sponsoring their secondary school, and they sit on their Canadian Board as well as their Advisory Board. A childhood sexual abuse survivor, Shantelle joined forces with Boost for Kids as Honorary Chair, and she shared her story as the guest speaker at their 2018 Butterfly Ball. Shantelle's life has been centered around children since she became pregnant with her first daughter at nineteen, so it is no surprise that her charitable endeavors focus primarily on kids in need.

📷 @shantellebisson

📷 @withoutlosingyourcool

🐦 @shantellebisson

f ShantelleBissonOfficial

🌐 www.shantellebisson.com

YGTMama Media Co. is a blended boutique publishing house for mission-driven humans. We help seasoned and emerging authors "birth their brain babies" through a supportive and collaborative approach. Specializing in narrative nonfiction and adult and children's empowerment books, we believe that words can change the world, and we intend to do so one book at a time.

www.ygtmama.com/publishing

@ygtmama.media.co

@ygtmama.media.co

Manufactured by Amazon.ca
Bolton, ON